HR for Line Managers
Best Practice

Frank Scott-Lennon
& Conor Hannaway

MANAGEMENT
BRIEFS

Essential Insights for Busy Managers

Acknowledgements

We are most grateful to many, many managers - too numerous to mention - within various organisations; their ideas and practice have greatly informed our thinking and our view of best practice.

We are also most grateful to those managers who read earlier drafts of this book and enriched us with their insights.

We particularly wish to thank our wives, Claire and Sinead. Without their continuing support, this book and all of our other work, would not be possible.

Frank Scott-Lennon
Conor Hannaway

November 2010

© 2010 by Frank Scott-Lennon and Conor Hannaway
First published in 2010
ISBN 978-1-906946-01-2

Production credits
All design, artwork and liaison with printers has been undertaken by Neworld Associates, 9 Greenmount Avenue, Harold's Cross, Dublin 12, www.neworld.com

Publisher: Management Briefs, 30 The Palms, Clonskeagh, Dublin 14.

Table of Contents

Foreword

This book should be most helpful to all line managers who wish to achieve Best Practice in the way in which they manage and achieve optimum performance for their people within their domains.

It is a very welcome addition to our developing series of Human Resource, Organisation Behaviour and General Management Books.

All of the books in the series aim to capture the essentials for busy Managers; essential knowledge and skill presented in an accessible and easy-to-read style.

A list of books already published within the series appears on the inside of the back cover. Also, on one of the last pages of the book, you will find a list of forthcoming titles which can also be viewed at our website www.ManagementBriefs.com.

We welcome any contact from you the reader; it will only improve our products and our connection to our reader population.

Frank Scott-Lennon
Series Editor
Frank@ManagementBriefs.com

November 2010

Introduction

Chapter outline

→ Importance of People Management in Today's World
→ Why Line Managers Should take the Lead
→ Key Elements of People Management
→ Simple and Uncomplicated 'Approaches and Systems'

Importance of People Management in Today's World

Managers are charged with the responsibility of achieving organisational goals. Organisations operate by breaking these goals down into specific tasks and responsibilities for individuals and teams.

It is not sufficient for a manager to focus on task/responsibility achievement alone, as if in a vacuum of technicality. All managers and team leaders must take account of the basic fact that such tasks and responsibilities are achieved through people.

Best Practice People Management is all the more required in today's complex organisations where higher levels of performance are repeatedly demanded and change is the only constant. It is critical that managers acquire the skills to manage the people in their teams as effectively as possible.

Why Line Managers Should take the Lead

It is not uncommon to hear managers say: "I'm here to get the job done and I don't have the time for people management; that is the responsibility of the HR Department!" Such thoughts, or more importantly the behaviours that follow them, have no place in Best Practice People Management.

Managers at the front end of task accomplishment are in the best position to manage staff well. They should not shirk this responsibility or leave it for someone else to do.

The manager must take full responsibility for both task and people management. Failure to manage both, will mean that the manager is not using the full armoury at his/her disposal.

Key Elements of People Management

Within this *HR for Line Managers - Best Practice* book, we present what we believe are the key Human Resource (HR) practices that make for excellent People Management.

We treat in turn each of the following topics:

→ Getting the Right People: Best Recruitment and Selection Practices

→ 'Settling in' new staff: Best Induction Practices

→ Probation

→ Managing Individual and Team Performance

→ Recognition and Reward

→ Employee Grievances

→ Handling Discipline

→ Learning and Development

→ Upholding Dignity and Respect in the Workplace

→ Change Management

→ Enhancing Personal Commitment of Staff

→ Positive Employee Relations

→ Culture as an aid to Organisational Strategy.

Most of the above topics are found in books written for HR professionals. However we approach all of them from the viewpoint of the essential know-how and skills that managers need to have so that they can:

→ Develop the HR skills required in today's world

→ Create a healthy HR culture within their team

→ Develop a close relationship with their team members

→ Maximise individual and team performance

→ Align team members with organisational goals.

Simple and Uncomplicated 'Approaches and Systems'

Throughout this book we have endeavoured to present approaches and systems that are uncomplicated. In doing so, we are driven by our desire to:

→ Create optimal learning transfer, and

→ Facilitate the application of the ideas in the workplace.

We hope that you the reader find that our thoughts and ideas do this for you.

We wish you well in your use of the ideas within this book!

1 Getting the Right People: Best Recruitment & Selection Practices

Chapter outline

→ Recruitment & Selection as an 'Inexact' Science
→ Establishing Selection Criteria
→ Gathering the Data at Interviews
→ Use of 'Scenario' Based Questioning
→ Note-taking at Interviews
→ First Impressions/Self-Justification
→ Data Comparison
→ Selection of Most Suitable Candidate
→ Post Selection Processes
→ Alternative Approaches

One of the manager's most important tasks is getting the right people who will fit into their team and make a significant contribution to organisational productivity. This responsibility is easier said than done. Selection effectively means being able to predict future performance based on quite limited information. In addition, there are a considerable number of procedural and legal challenges in picking the right person. However, the process set out in this chapter, should make it somewhat easier for managers to tackle this important task.

Recruitment & Selection as an 'Inexact' Science

At the outset, we should indicate that the selection of people is a very inexact science and managers are likely to make more mistakes in this realm of their decision making than in most others. The processes described in this chapter are aimed at trying to make recruitment and selection processes more exact. Although there is a wide range of techniques available to managers to help them identify the best candidate, this chapter focuses on the interview as the core technique for identifying the three essential tests:

→ Can the candidate do the job?

→ Will the candidate do the job?

→ Will the candidate fit into the team?

Establishing Selection Criteria

In order to achieve better results in selection managers must put some preparation into clarifying:

→ The precise job to be done, expressed as key responsibilities

→ The job context including flexibility, travel and location

→ The knowledge/skills and personal attitude/behaviours required

→ The attributes required of the new person to fit into the existing team.

Once the manager has completed the above he or she is then in a position to establish the selection criteria, **that is the criteria on which the selection decision will actually be made.**

Clarifying these selection criteria in advance of conducting any interviews facilitates a more systematic approach to the interview and the consequent selection decision. These selection criteria are used to develop questions/scenarios for candidates to enable the manager gather specific evidence with which to evaluate candidates. A sample set of selection criteria for a Production Team Leader is shown within Panel 1.1 opposite.

Panel 1.1

Possible Selection Criteria for Production Team Leader

Key responsibilities	Job context	Knowledge and skills	Team membership
Planning and organising	Prepared to work unsocial hours	Production planning skills	Shares the values
Technical assessment	Some travel required	Technical know-how/3rd level qualification	Enjoys team environment
Operational effectiveness		Completer/finisher	
Team Leadership		Team Leading Skills	
Quality		ISO training or Six Sigma experience	

Gathering the Data at Interview

The interview is then about gathering data against each of the criteria that have been established for a particular job — it is not just a cosy chat! Thus in respect of the Production Team Leader above the interviewer(s) will search for evidence within the various candidates' previous expertise and experience that would demonstrate their level of knowledge/skill against each of the criteria. The interviewer(s) should take notes of particular pieces of evidence that come out of the conversation with the candidates.

Use of 'Scenario' Based Questioning

When deciding on the actual questions to ask candidates, it is useful to develop scenarios/real life situations which the successful applicant might face. All candidates should be asked the same scenario based questions. The different responses allow the interviewer/panel to see how individual candidates are going to react to particular situations that they might have to deal with in their jobs.

There are many similarities between what we are describing as scenario based interviewing and the competency based approach being used by many organisations.

In competency based interviews, the interviewer asks each candidate a set of questions around each competency (further information on competencies is outlined in Chapter 5). The candidate is asked about a time when he or she has had to use a particular competency. "Tell me about a time when you had to deal with a particular situation, (e.g. handle a difficult customer)" The follow-up questions are:

→ What was the situation?

→ What did you do?

→ What was the outcome?

→ What did you learn that might be of advantage in the position we are discussing?

In Panel 1.2 you can see an example of how some of the selection criteria were questioned and responded to during an interview.

Panel 1.2

Sample Interview Questions

Selection criteria	Question	Contrasting responses
Planning and organising	Tell me about a time when you had to make a deadline	"In my last job, there were frequent breakdowns in the assembly area. The packer and I would often stay till mid-night to get the product out."
Team leading	Tell me about a time when you had to manage conflict between team members	"I recall an occasion when two team members got into a row over a work station and I had to facilitate....."
Travel between centres	How do you feel about having to travel?	"I have no problem with travelling. Part of my last job involved Sales and I had to visit customers every week"

Scenarios are mostly used where the person is being considered for a role they have not performed before whilst the competency approach is used to show how they used their knowledge and skills in the past. Essentially the process is the same for both approaches.

→ Key competencies are identified

→ Data is gathered using the scenario/incident/caselet approach

→ Candidates are compared on the basis of the data gathered.

Note-taking at Interviews

Whatever the method used it is important to keep sufficiently adequate notes during interviews and at the decision stage so that:

→ There is a clear linkage between the data and the decision

→ This linkage can be explained to any candidates seeking feedback regarding their performance at the interview.

Notes may also be required in the event of an appeal of the outcome of the selection process or in the event of legal action being taken in respect of the selection decision.

Panel 1.3

Getting the Best from Selection Interviews

→ Prepare well by establishing clear selection criteria.

→ Put candidates at ease.

→ Utilise scenarios/caselets to gather evidence on competencies.

→ Utilise key interviewing skills, such as:

- Active listening
- Be wary of First Impressions — they are usually gathered on the basis of flimsy evidence
- Avoid Self-Justification where one incorrectly builds on First Impressions to reinforce inaccurate conclusions
- Use open-ended, probing and reflective questions, as appropriate.

→ Allow an opportunity for candidates to ask questions and put forward any issues that they wish to discuss.

→ Summarise the place of the interview in the recruitment process and inform the candidate of the next steps in the selection process.

First Impressions/ Self-Justification

Before leaving interviewing we should stress that interviewers should **not** allow First Impressions to influence their judgements too heavily. One of the great difficulties with First Impressions is that they are very often gleaned from flimsy evidence. They can become quite rigid assessments of a person's suitability for a position. The problem is made worse by a tendency for the interviewer to look for data that will support those impressions in a Self-Justificatory process, rather than looking for data that will challenge them. Therefore it is important for interviewers to realise the power of both First Impressions and Self-Justification and to be wary that they are not misled by such tendencies.

Data Comparison

Once all of the interviews for a particular position have been completed, it is necessary to compare the data from the interviews in such a way that each candidate is evaluated against each of the independent criteria. This may bring about a situation where candidate A is ahead of candidate B on one criteria but further back on another. The process allows interviewers to look at all candidates across each of the criteria rather than just looking at them as a whole. The simple form within Panel 1.4 below may aid this process; the example used within the Panel 1.4 is for a Production Team Leader position.

Panel 1.4
Sample form for Comparison of Candidates

Selection criteria	Below standard	Meets standard	Excels
Technical Knowledge	PJ	JB TJ	
Project Approach to Tasks		JB PJ TJ	
Quality		PJ	JB TJ
Team Leading Skills	PJ	JB TJ	
Completer/Finisher Mode		PJ JB	TJ
'Fit' with job context		PJ JB	TJ
'Fit' with team		PJ JB TJ	

Utilising a process similar to the above, facilitates interviewers as they rate the candidates against the selection criteria. Each candidate is rigorously assessed against each criterion before a decision is made.

Selection of Most Suitable Candidate

Resulting from the comparison of data above, the manager is then in a position to select the most suitable candidate. In some instances the 'best' candidate may not in fact be the most suitable.

For example, one candidate might really outscore others on several of the criteria but on the most critical one, for example Team Leading Skills, he or she may fall down. Therefore it is important to weight the criteria prior to the interview process or certainly prior to the comparison of candidates. One of the simplest ways to give weights to different criteria is to describe them as desirable, essential or distinguishing. The latter characteristic refers to criteria that are not only essential but would make, in the case of an employee who excels in them, a significant difference to future job performance.

Post Selection Processes

Once a candidate has been selected, then one of the interviewers or another person in the organisation should carry out the various reference checks. This is best done by contact with individual referees either in person or on the telephone rather than through the printed word, as written references often do not reflect an accurate picture of the candidate's ability.

It will also be necessary at this stage to arrange for the successful candidate to go through a medical examination appropriate to the position so that you can be sure that the person is fit to do the job.

Once a Letter of Appointment has been prepared, the successful candidate should be asked to visit the organisation again; the purpose of this visit is for the direct line manager responsible for the new employee to make the actual offer of employment. Doing things this way helps cement the relationship between the two of them. It also allows it be seen as clearly being between the two of them – this is an important initial bonding process.

Panel 1.5

Letter of Appointment

A letter of appointment needs to be prepared, it should include at least:

→ Job offer

→ Job title/key responsibilities

→ Starting date

→ Hours and place of work

→ Any special requirements such as driving licence

→ Probation period

→ Salary

→ Holiday entitlements

→ Notice period

→ Any other 'perks' such as pension, health insurance

→ A reference to attached terms and conditions of employment to be signed by the potential new staff member

Panel 1.5 (contd)

→ Brief outline of employee grievance and disciplinary procedures

→ An expression of confidence in the person in their new role and a 'welcome' to the organisation

The letter usually sets out arrangements regarding medical examinations and reference checking.

It should also be emphasised that organisations need to bring the best values of customer service to the job of releasing unsuccessful candidates. This process should be done only after a full written acceptance from the successful candidate. The words chosen should not in any way damage the self-esteem of those candidates and the process should be as warm and friendly as possible.

Alternative Approaches

The above recruitment and selection process is suitable for internal or external selection competitions.

It should be noted that there are other alternative approaches to recruitment and selection such as:

→ Open recruitment days where the initial screening of a large number of candidates could be undertaken by a group of managers

→ The use of Recruitment Agencies where a percentage fee (usually 15 to 25 percent) is charged for submitting a shortlist of potentially suitable candidates

→ The use of Assessment Centres where candidates are put through a number of organisational specific exercises similar to a work situation likely to be faced by the successful candidate.

It was stated at the outset of this chapter that recruitment and selection is an inexact science and we would like to close by repeating that and saying that the use of the processes described within this chapter should greatly help a manager in getting more of the right people into the organisation.

Summary of Chapter 1

→ Selecting staff is a key role for managers, particularly in today's world when expertise, productivity and flexibility are so important

→ Recruitment and selection is an inexact science

→ Build the interview process around selection criteria and/ or competencies

→ Use scenarios/caselets to gather data against criteria/ competencies

→ Try to put off judgement
during data gathering

→ Do not be swayed by
First Impressions or
Self-Justification

→ Keep adequate notes during
interview and when comparing
candidates

→ When the decision is made use
good follow-up procedures,
including reference checks and
medical examination

→ Make the job offer in as
personal a manner as possible,
preferably face-to-face

→ Release non-successful
candidates in a customer
friendly manner and with a
warm 'thank you' for their time.

2

'Settling In' New Staff – Best Induction Practices

Chapter outline

→ Initial Entry and Socialisation Processes

→ 'Buddying' or 'Angel' Approaches

→ The Psychological Contract

→ Focusing the Job Performance of the New Employee

→ Envelop New Employees with Organisational Values

→ Induction is a Far Bigger Process than the Training Room

→ Topics to be Included in the Induction Process

Initial Entry and Socialisation Processes

The hiring manager has seen his/her relationship develop through the interview process and the making of the offer of employment. It is important to develop that relationship when the employee comes into the organisation, particularly in the early days/weeks of employment. The line manager has a major task in helping the new staff member to settle into the organisation. If this is done correctly, there will be further enhancement of the relationship between the two individuals.

Many organisations further this socialisation process by appointing a 'buddy' or 'angel' for new staff. It is the task of these individuals to ensure that they stay close to the new employee and are able to answer any queries they have about the organisation, the people and/or its processes.

One of the first things that a manager should do, in preparation for the newly starting team member, is to ensure that all necessary supports are in place, such as:

- PC and relevant accessories
- Email set up in advance
- Phone extension fully sorted
- Swipe card

Some managers may feel that these are the responsibility of someone else in the organisation, but our point is that they should work in advance of the arrival of a new team member to ensure that they are all fully in place. Doing so will ensure a smooth transition into the organisation for the new team member.

The socialisation process at work, particularly in this early period, is of great importance. The hiring manager should encourage and help the integration of new team members into the existing team and should ensure that they are not left alone at important times such as break times and lunch periods.

'Buddying' or 'Angel' Approaches

Many organisations further this socialisation process by appointing a 'buddy' or 'angel' for new staff. It is the task of these individuals to ensure that they stay close to the new employee and are able to answer any queries they have about the organisation, the people and/or its processes. Systems such as these greatly aid the settling-in process and also ensure that there is an immediate connection available for answering any queries.

The Psychological Contract

A psychological contract defines the expectations that the organisation has regarding how new team members will go about their jobs. It covers areas such as productivity, quality, safety, customer service and team working. The quid pro quo of this contract relates to issues of concern to the team member such as management style, respect for the individual, involvement, the support they can expect and job security. The team leader should see herself/himself in a fully supportive role so to ensure engagement in and delivery of the terms of such a contract.

Focusing the Job Performance of the New Employee

The importance of Performance Management is stressed in a later chapter of this book. However, let us emphasise now that it comes into play in the very early stages of employment. As well as working out the precise role for the individual, both team leader and particularly the new employee need to clarify their expectations of the role. This is best achieved through:

→ Focusing the new employee on the critical areas of the job — Key Result Areas (KRAs)

→ Setting some goals where they can see achievement against these KRAs.

We should say that the identification of KRAs and goal-setting is an ongoing interactive process. This process works best when it includes a two-way discussion in a supportive environment. It is not achieved by just handing over a document such as a job description. It requires on-going discussion to ensure maximum clarity and acceptance.

Envelop New Employees with Organisational Values

Very often new employees are sufficiently left to their own devices that they either introduce values that they bring with them or they absorb values haphazardly within the organisation. We strongly believe that managers and team leaders should envelop new employees as far as possible within a strong value system. Thus, if the organisation is focusing on team work, quality and customer service then such managers should provide employees with clear experiences that shape their attitude to these values. The most successful way of doing this, particularly in the

19

early stages of employment, is to provide these new employees with opportunities for involvement in activities and projects that embody the values in practice. New employees are then able to see the importance that the organisation places on such values.

Induction is a Far Bigger Process than the Training Room

In conclusion we say that induction is a far bigger process than the traditional training room approach. We hope that we have inspired the reader to see the benefits of a multi-faceted approach so that they will be committed to work on these various initiatives; if they do, both the manager and the new team member will benefit from the relationship building effects referred to above.

Many elements of the formal induction process are usually provided by HR although more and more of this responsibility is being given to Line Managers. We outline in Panel 2.1 below those elements that need to be covered within an induction programme.

Panel 2.1
Topics to be Included in the Induction Process

→ Vision and values

→ Health and Safety

→ Operating practices

→ Key policies

→ Dignity at Work Policy

→ Policy for the Internet

→ Payment of Wages and Overtime

→ Pensions

→ Health Insurance

→ Grievance Handling

→ Discipline Handling

There are in today's world many software packages that focus on induction with the dual benefit that the individual can access the information themselves on a need-to-know basis. Many organisations are now modifying such packages in order to deliver more and more of the traditional training room approach to induction.

Summary of Chapter 2

→ Managers should play a key pro-active part in the early socialisation processes for new employees

→ Many organisations further this socialisation process through using a 'buddy' or 'angel'

→ Local managers/team leaders should focus on building a psychological contract that engages new employees and brings them towards their optimum contribution

→ Performance expectations of both the new employee and manager/team leader need attention in this early phase

→ New employees need to be encouraged to work on projects that will build behaviours that are consistent with organisational values

→ Traditional induction information should be given on a need to know basis and software packages are helpful in this regard

→ Successful induction is an on-going activity for managers/team leaders, not just a training room process.

3 Probation

Chapter outline

→ Role of Probation Process
→ Earning *Respect* and *Trust*
→ Coaching
→ Performance Development
→ Performance Review
→ Review of Progress /
    Decision to Retain or Let Go
→ Manager's Tasks when Approaching
    Probation End

Role of Probation Process

Within the last chapter we stressed the opportunity that the manager has for developing a relationship with all new team members; such managers should live the values of the organisation and attempt to inculcate them into all new employees. The probation period, offers an opportunity over a reasonably extended period of time, to see whether the new employee is able to live up to the requirements of the position and to fulfil expectations in line with the psychological contract which was discussed in the last chapter.

The first step is for the manager to earn the respect and trust of the new employee so that performance discussions can be conducted in the best environment. The probation period can be difficult for new employees who are aware that if they fail to perform satisfactorily, may have their employment terminated.

The first step is for the manager to earn the respect and trust of the new employee so that performance discussions can be conducted in the best environment.

Earning *Respect* and *Trust*

In the first instance managers are the people who must earn the respect and trust of team members.

Panel 3.1

4 Tips for Earning Respect and Trust

1 Identify small ways in which you can provide resources or support which the individual requires

2 Specify the detail and when you'll get it done

3 Strive to ensure full delivery inside the time frame

4 Ensure that your behaviour is consistent over time so that the new employee will grow to respect and trust you – they will see you are a person of your word.

Note

Completing 1 & 2 above but not 3 will demonstrate a failure to follow through; this will have the opposite to the intended effect and will leave individuals/teams lacking in respect and trust for you.

Coaching

Coaching skills are of critical importance for managers. Like coaches in sport, managers in organisations must develop a skill set that enables them to bring out the best from team members. Not all managers are endowed with the same level of coaching skills. Panel 3.2 shows ways in which they can enhance their competence as coaches by working on the sub-skills described.

Panel 3.2

Sub-Skills of Coaching

→ Develop alertness in seeking issues/skills that provide an opportunity for coaching

→ Devise with team member a way forward perhaps albeit in a staged manner

→ Provide necessary support that facilitates the development of the skill

→ Review improvements with the team member and encourage further growth.

Performance Development

Two of the most important building blocks of performance development are:

→ Helping new employees see the contribution they can make

→ Building their confidence around their abilities

In the wider team/organisation context, it is also important that the manager ensures that they help the problem employee overcome any efforts by others to:

→ Prevent their full contribution being given

→ Slowing down work processes, or

→ Working against the team values

Performance Review

Once the two most important building blocks are put in place, the manager must utilise their own performance management techniques to sit down with employees on probation in order to assess their progress against:

→ Shared expectations, and

→ Jointly agreed goals

The manager must then provide the coaching and feedback discussion that will review progress and support the drive for ever-improving performance.

Review of Progress/ Decision to Retain or Let Go

This ongoing performance development and progress review should lead to a situation that, at least one month prior to the end of the probation, the manager can decide whether or not he or she wish to:

→ Confirm employment

→ Extend the probation

→ 'Let go'

In fairness to both parties, there should be a rigorous and thorough process along the lines shown within Panel 3.3 below.

Failure to take the above process seriously will lead to unsatisfactory employees 'slipping through the net', as it were. They will then be much more difficult to mould or change after that.

In conclusion, the probation period is a critical opportunity for a manager in developing relationships and the performance of individuals. It gives the manager an opportunity to build sound relationships for the future and to put in place a robust performance management system that will serve both parties well in future years.

Panel 3.3

Manager's Tasks when Approaching Probation End

→ Thoroughly review performance against expectations

→ Check growth of individual

→ Review how employee 'fits in' with colleagues

→ Formally assess flexibility and openness to change

→ Talk with colleague managers regarding their views

→ Review all of the above with employee

→ Confirm employment, extend probation as appropriate or terminate.

Summary of Chapter 3

→ Earning respect and trust is vital — so deliver on your commitments!

→ Develop good Coaching Skills

→ Help individuals to clearly see the contribution they can make

→ Build employee confidence in their skills and ability

→ The manager should clarify performance expectations with key members and coach them to enhanced performance, providing regular feedback on progress

→ Finally review all aspects of employees contribution at least one month prior to probation end

→ Utilise the relationship building approaches of probation and Performance Development techniques that will be useful for both parties in the future.

4

Managing Individual and Team Performance

Chapter outline

→ Managing Performance is a Key Responsibility for All Managers

→ The D E F T Model is helpful for Managing Performance:
  - Dialogue
  - Expectations
  - Feedback
  - Timely Approach

→ Meaningful Dialogue About Job Responsibilities

→ Expectations and 'Line of Sight' to Organisational Goals

→ Key Result Areas

→ Jointly-driven Process

→ Goal-setting

→ Personal Development of the Individual and Competency Development

→ Tips for Giving Feedback

→ Timely Approach

→ Reviewing Poor Performance

Managing Performance is a Key Responsibility for All Managers

For maximum effectiveness each managers should have a robust Performance Management System (PMS) that delivers clarity about what needs to be done — we call this his/her PMS. Having a robust personal system of PMS is more important than any centralised HR driven PMS. Such a personal system does not have to be complex — indeed it can as simple as the DEFT model treated below.

The DEFT Model is Helpful for Managing Performance

D – Dialogue
E – Expectations
F – Feedback
T – Timely Approach

Meaningful Dialogue about Job Responsibilities

DIALOGUE is at the core of the PMS process. The dialogue between each manager and his/her direct report is the most critical part of successful management. The candour and honesty of this dialogue is at the core of successful performance management. The initial dialogue meeting is perhaps the most important part of our model of performance management; this is the first opportunity for the planning of goal achievement and personal development. It is vitally important because, at this initial stage, we would stress that performance management has very, very little to do with the completion of forms. Research suggests that circa 50% of performance management systems are **not** effective. This finding is largely due to the fact that they are form focused and what are called 'tick and flick' systems. This view usually reflects the fact that the process is seen as an 'add-on' by line management rather than an integral part of how they manage their own people.

An effective system on the other hand has everything to do with creating a climate for meaningful dialogue between a manager and team member at the commencement of a performance management review period and during same. Some managers suggest that within their busy jobs they do not have time for the level of dialogue required. In fact, it is often these very managers who are likely to need it most. However, every manager must understand that his/her core role is to achieve results through and with people and to build the capability of each employee and the team; this may only be achieved through meaningful dialogue.

Having a robust personal system of PMS is more important than any centralised HR driven PMS.

Panel 4.1

Sample Dialogue at Outset of PMS

→ Arrange initial meeting with team member

→ Explore business and organisation realities and identify the personal contribution required over the coming period within the particular organisation/department/section

→ Indicate that one wishes to utilise DEFT as a focusing process

→ Briefly explain components of DEFT and demonstrate how it can be linked to business direction

→ Stress that it is not about form filling — any paperwork/form used is simply a record of commitment to each other

→ Ask the individual to explore what they can contribute to achieving the requirements for the section and explore how they need to change their behaviours and develop new competencies to achieve these requirements

→ Ask the individual to review their career aspirations and plans

→ Suggest a meeting the following week to discuss from both viewpoints — Key Result Areas and Goals.

Expectations and 'Line of Sight' to Organisational Goals

EXPECTATIONS about the requirements of the job are the principal subject matter for this dialogue between the line manager and his/her team member. Every effort should be made to clarify the expectations that each has in respect of the job that is required to be done. Goals should be constructed in a manner that shows a clear 'line of sight' to organisational strategies, values and goals.

Key Result Areas

KRAs are those parts of a job where performance is required and where the greatest contribution is made. Examples of KRAs for a Production Manager are listed in Panel 4.2.

> **Panel 4.2**
>
> # Sample KRAs Production Manager
>
> → Output – product/service
>
> → Quality – product/service
>
> → Wastage/re-work
>
> → Lean initiatives
>
> → Teamwork commitments
>
> → Materials

> **Panel 4.2 (contd)**
>
> → MIS/OIS
>
> → Budgets
>
> → Empowerment
>
> → Performance Management
>
> ⟩ Process controls
>
> → Communication

Jointly-driven Process

As indicated earlier when treating dialogue above, it is imperative that this process is essentially a jointly-driven process. As we will show later, this process revolves principally around the establishment of the Key Result Areas (KRAs) for the job and the goals that are to be attained within each of those KRAs.

Goal-setting

Goals are the ways in which performance is directed and measured. The most effective goals follow the SMART formula, i.e. they are Specific, Measurable, Achievable, Relevant and Time-based. Managers find it fairly easy to develop SMART goals for KRAs such as sales, production and finance. Panel 4.3 gives some tips for developing goals within KRAs where it is more difficult to construct goals.

Panel 4.3

Tips for Goal-setting within Difficult KRAs

Take for example a context where a manager wants to set some goals within the KRA of Teamwork. As he or she initially approaches this task it may appear difficult to write specific goals.

Then ..... stop the clock, as it were, ... and pick up those areas in which things might go wrong if one was not attending to teamwork.

Think specifically of what we would see (the actual visible behaviours).

This process might generate issues such as:

→ lack of direction within the team

→ duplication or overlapping of tasks

→ interpersonal conflicts within the team

→ poor 'customer service' behaviours

It is then possible to set goals in some or all the above which will undoubtedly contribute to an improvement in teamwork.

Note: This technique is not alone useful for a blank that one might have with qualitative KRAs but the technique is also useful with quantitative KRAs.

Personal Development of the Individual and Competency Development

Performance planning discussions should focus, not only on performance, but also on the competencies required for the successful execution of performance plans. Accordingly competency development and the personal development of the individual should be addressed and recorded as part of the plan. This focus can lead towards setting jointly agreed goals for knowledge/ skill attainment. Some of our best development comes through identifying specific job and personal competencies which need development. A more complete schema for competency and personal development is included in Chapter 8 of this book.

Tips for Giving Feedback

FEEDBACK is an essential ingredient for a good PMS. In its simplest terms, it is an opportunity for both parties to explore how they believe the team member is performing against the expectations that have been clarified earlier; it also provides an opportunity for discussing progress against these expectations on a regular basis and for focusing on the personal development of the team member.

Panel 4.5

Key Tips in Giving Feedback for Reviewers

→ Reviewing and Preparing: There is no substitute for being well-prepared in advance of a performance feedback session. The foundation of the preparation is in looking back on performance (the results achieved and the behaviours demonstrated) within the review period with particular focus on the goals and competencies/behaviours that were agreed at the outset.

→ Focus on Personal Development: The performance discussion must have a component within which there is a full discussion of the personal development requirements and possibilities (competency development) for the reviewee.

→ Follow-through: Good follow-up mechanisms are critical on those actions that have been agreed about both performance and personal development. Managers who do not deliver on promised follow-through in this regard lose the trust of their staff.

Panel 4.6

Key Skills of Feedback for Reviewees

→ Reviewing and Preparing: Reviewees need to develop the skill of dispassionately examining their own performance over the review period with particular reference to the agreed goals. Within this preparation, they should practice the skill of reviewing: *'What went well, and why?'* and *'What could be improved, and how?'*

→ Listening and Assertiveness: Reviewees need to be able to listen well in as non-defensive a mode as possible and also to be

Panel 4.6 (contd)

able to assert their own view of performance in a non-aggressive mode. These two skills are core elements of influencing.

→ Self-Analysing: It is important that reviewees are capable of critical

self-analysis in respect of their own performance and personal development needs. If they are so capable, they will be able to present an accurate view of themselves in a developmental context.

Timely Approach

TIMELY treatment of each of the above elements of the PMS is critical. Thus the clarification of expectations should be undertaken at a meaningful time within the business cycle of the organisation. It is also important that feedback is not given in a quick once-a-year setting but is a regular part of the dialogue that should take place between team leader and team member. If this is not happening on an on-going basis, the PMS will not be effective.

The effective PMS then is reflected in how we personally manage It is not an 'add on' form filling exercise. If the manager contracts effectively with the employee and then plans the formal and informal dialogues, he or she will begin to manage through the PMS process rather than add the process to how he or she manages. Effectively handled he or she can save valuable management time through this investment in good management practice.

Reviewing Poor Performance

Panel 4.7

Tips for Reviewing Poor Performance

→ Focus the employee on the overall organisational goals

→ Seek employee's view of any dip in performance

→ Contribute your view as to possible causes

→ Re-focus the employee on original or amended goals

→ Clarify any support/ coaching that you need to provide

→ Agree further short-term review(s) of performance

Most of what we stated above has referred to reviewing the performance of individuals. It is however an easy jump for the reader to see that everything that has been said about managing the performance of individuals equally applies to how we go about managing the performance of a team. Thus the DEFT model is eminently suitable to aid the management of performance within teams whether they are high-performing or are performing below expectations.

Summary of Chapter 4

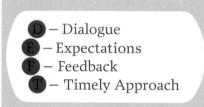

→ To be fully effective, managers must develop their own personal Personal Performance Management System (PMS) for use with team members

→ D E F T is the model for successful PMS — At its core are Dialogue, Expectations & Feedback. All must be completed in a Timely manner

→ Dialogue is at the heart of the process; it involves 'engaging' and explaining the essentials for job/role success. Candour and open communication are at the core of good dialogue

→ Expectations, when well clarified through KRAs and goals, give motivational direction and provide the context for performance improvement in the period ahead

→ A clear line of sight to organisational goals must be maintained when setting individual and team goals

→ Feedback must be regular and focused on performance against expectations and also on skill/competency enhancement

→ Timely treatment of each of the above elements is critical - PMS must become part of 'how we manage' day by day, month by month....not just a 'once-a-year' exercise

→ All of the above should be part of our personal 'way of managing'

→ Your personal PMS can be used for teams as well as individuals.

Recognition and Reward

5

Chapter outline

→ How Rewards Work
→ What to Reward
→ How to Reward
→ Rewarding Performance Throughout
   the Year
→ Recognising Effective Performance
→ Using Informal Rewards
→ Responding to Higher Level Needs

Two of the most important tools in a manager's toolkit are goal-setting and recognising performance. Goal-setting gets people working in the right direction and knowing what they are trying to achieve. Recognising good performance reinforces the successful behaviours of team members and encourages them to keep up the good work.

Research into what motivates people at work shows that recognition is a vital element in high performance organisations. However, employee surveys consistently demonstrate that lack of recognition is the single greatest source of dissatisfaction that people experience in organisations.

Managers sometimes have a limited view of the range of possibilities for rewarding staff. Too often they have difficulty in knowing how best to recognise performance. One thing is clear. Managers should not rely on salary increments or annual bonuses alone.

This chapter sets out a comprehensive range of techniques that managers can use to recognise and reward performance without relying on the organisation's remuneration system. However, before looking at them, it is useful to understand some of the basic ground-rules governing the use of rewards.

How Rewards Work

Some managers dispute the need for rewards. They say that their staff are paid to turn up for work and to do a good job. They say that they will deal with employees who do not perform well with some form of corrective action. These managers fail to recognise the following important dimensions of employee performance:

→ Even the least effective employees learn where the threshold of poor performance lies

→ Acceptable performance can range from being satisfactory to outstanding and the manager needs to understand how to encourage team members to strive to the highest performance levels

→ Employees are highly sensitive to equity and, if they think that their extra efforts are not being recognised, they will frequently lower their performance so that it corresponds with the recognition they receive.

The first thing managers need to think about is the performance they wish to reward. Managers should be explicit with their team members regarding the performance that they will be rewarding. They will find it easier to use rewards when they talk regularly to their team members about performance issues. There are many times when this conversation can take place, such as when staff are joining their organisation, during performance planning sessions and at team meetings. Panel 5.1 gives some examples of the performance areas that a manager can discuss.

Panel 5.1

What to Reward

The fairest way to go about rewarding staff is to explain to them in advance about the performance which is required. There are four main areas which managers can focus on.

Goal achievement: When goals are set in advance, the manager should be on the lookout for when goals are achieved and immediately recognise the team member's success. Care should be taken to ensure that team members do not achieve their success through focusing on some goals at the expense of others.

Honest endeavour: Sometimes, due to circumstances outside the control of team members, a goal will not be achieved despite their best efforts. In these situations, managers should consider recognising the contribution of team members so as to encourage future performance. This process is particularly important when a team member takes on a particularly difficult assignment.

Special effort: Even when goals are not set in advance, a team member may make a special effort at personal expense to achieve a result or to deal with a crisis. It is vital that managers respond to these situations so that team members know that special efforts are seen and appreciated.

Values and behaviours: This factor can be summarised by the phrase: 'it ain't what you do but the way that you do it'. Sometimes team members are so driven by their goals, particularly if they know that they will be rewarded, that they forget the most important values of the organisation and behave in an inappropriate manner. It is important that team members understand that goal achievement is not a success if it is done at the expense of organisation values such as quality, customer service or teamwork. Work behaviours like time-keeping, attendance, adherence to safety standards and demonstrating flexibility also need to be factored in.

How to Reward

How is it that some organisations with generous rewards packages fail to attain high levels of performance? The answer is quite simple. They do not apply a few simple ground rules that must be followed if rewards are to have the desired effect. Failure to follow the rules can result not only in wasted resources but in disillusionment and cynicism amongst all employees. One important point to note is that rewards fall into two major categories.

The first category may be called extrinsic rewards, such as salary increases, bonuses etc. They tend to have a relatively short-term value when compared to intrinsic rewards where effective performers experience job satisfaction associated with challenging and developmental work assignments. Panel 5.2 sets out ten guidelines to help managers ensure that their rewards have the right impact on employee performance.

Panel 5.2

Rewarding with Impact

❶ Team members should know in advance the goals and behaviours that will be rewarded. Managers should spend time with their staff explaining how performance and rewards are linked.

❷ Team members should believe that the goals are achievable. Managers should bear in mind that team members will often give up on goals that they do not think they can achieve.

❸ The rewards should be proportionate to the effort and skills which the team member has to apply in achieving the required levels of performance. The rule applies mostly to end of year rewards. On-going recognition can be more modest.

❹ Team members will adjust their performance if they do not feel that the reward system is equitable. They will keep a close watch on how other team members are treated and will respond accordingly.

❺ The rewards must be valued by the team members. No amount of a reward, which team members do not want, is going to motivate them. Some team members want extrinsic rewards. Others value intrinsic rewards.

Panel 5.2 (contd)

6 The most powerful reinforcement of performance is personal recognition by the manager. Catch team members doing something right and tell them immediately.

7 Recognition works best when it occurs soon after the event. Rewards work best when they occur at irregular intervals. This rule is one of the reasons why annual salary review and bonuses have limited value for most employees in organisations.

8 Be aware of the "Folly of Rewarding A, when Desiring B". Sometimes the wrong behaviours are rewarded. For example, paying too much overtime can result in slower work or restrictive practices as team members come to rely on these additional payments.

9 Withholding rewards from poor performers, such as not applying a salary increment, does not have as strong a motivational impact as giving rewards to high performers.

10 Be aware of playing favourites and make sure that everyone has an equal chance of having their performance recognised.

Rewarding Performance Throughout the Year

The formalistic approach to rewards in some organisations fails to have the desired impact. As can be seen from Panel 5.2 above, salary increments and bonuses seldom adhere to the guidelines for rewarding staff in ways that impact on performance on an on-going basis. Managers need to use a wider palette of rewards in order to create a high performance organisation. In particular, recognition and rewards need to move from being a periodic activity to being more evenly spread throughout the year.

Recognising Effective Performance

There are many different ways in which managers can recognise effective performance by individual team members or by the whole team, as shown in Panel 5.3 overleaf.

Managers need to use a wider palette of rewards in order to create a high performance organisation

Panel 5.3

Ten Ways to Recognise Effective Performance

1. Visit their workplace and personally thank team members face-to-face

2. Write to the team member and put a note on his/her file

3. Send a letter to the team member at his/her family home

4. Mention the performance of the individual at a team meeting or at a company event

5. Put a notice on the notice board

6. Ask your manager to write to the team member thanking him/her for their performance

7. Put an article in the organisation's newsletter

8. Allow team members to present their work to higher levels of management or include their achievement in training events

9. Enter their achievement for an award

10. Use the achievement in promotional events or annual reports.

Using Informal Rewards

Managers have much more discretion to reward team members than they may think. It sometimes takes a little effort to identify ways that are meaningful to team members. They will appreciate a manager's genuine efforts. Sometimes it is the thought that counts. Panel 5.4 sets out a number of informal rewards which managers can use on an on-going basis.

Managers have much more discretion to reward team members than they may think. It sometimes takes a little effort to identify ways that are meaningful to team members.

43

Panel 5.4

Using Informal Rewards

1 Buy a cake or some goodies to enjoy in the workplace

2 Hold a social event to celebrate the team's success

3 Allow some of the savings/increased earnings to be used to develop the work of the team

4 Give the team member time-off or allow him/her to finish early

5 Arrange a team visit to a centre of excellence

6 Put up a plaque or photograph to mark the team's achievement

7 Improve the working environment, such as by re-decorating it or by improving the HVAC

8 Provide additional equipment or resources which they have been looking for

9 Make a donation or do some work for the charity of their choice

10 Solve some problem for the individual or the team or remove a blockage to their performance.

Responding to Higher Level Needs

Effective performance should provide the context for team member development and progression. Exceptional performance may enable managers to identify the potential in team members who are able to contribute at a higher level or in a different way. For many employees, personal and career development are the most important factors determining their satisfaction in work. Panel 5.5 sets out a number of ways in which managers can respond to effective performance in ways that are most meaningful for staff.

Effective performance should provide the context for team member development and progression.

Panel 5.5

Linking Performance with Progression

1 Explore developmental opportunities for team members with effective performance

2 Ensure that effective performance and poor performance are taken into account in selection and promotional decisions

3 Managers can provide personal coaching to effective performers enabling them to progress in their work

4 Effective performers could be given time-off to devote to some personal project

5 Review the role and job title of high performers as they take on additional responsibilities

6 Give high performers access to facilities that they would not normally be able to use

7 Send high performers on training programmes to enable them to make best use of their talents or to prepare for career advancement

8 Facilitate meetings between high performers and people with expertise or know-how who are role models or exemplars for team members

9 Provide books or elearning materials with which they can increase their competencies

10 Arrange a mentor for high performers to help them develop their careers.

Ultimately, managers who can respond to the higher level needs of their team members will have no difficulty in creating a high performance organisation as they enter a virtuous circle of performance and development.

This chapter has looked at how managers can use recognition and reward on an an-going basis to reinforce effective behaviour. None of the highlighted techniques and skills are rocket science and they are all easily accessible to managers committed to the development of high performance teams.

Summary of Chapter 5

→ Rewards work by reinforcing effective performance

→ Managers need to be clear with team members about the performance and the behaviours which they will reward

→ Managers need to be aware of the ten guidelines which determine whether rewards will have the right effect - see Panel 5.2

→ Managers should try to make recognition and reward operate on an on-going basis rather than as a once-a year-event

→ There are many different ways in which a manager can recognise effective performance − see Panel 5.3

→ Managers should develop a repertoire of informal rewards with which to reinforce the performance of team members and their teams − see Panel 5.4

→ Responding to higher level needs can create a virtuous circle of performance and development.

Employee Grievances

6

Chapter outline

→ Distinction between Complaint and Grievance

→ Ownership of Employee Grievances

→ Grievances are Felt More in the 'Gut' than in the 'Head'

→ Resolve Grievances at Lowest Level Possible

→ Resolve Grievances as Speedily as Possible

→ Grievance Structures and Processes

→ Consistency of Approach is Critical

→ Proactive Approaches to Grievance Resolution

Distinction between Complaint and Grievance

Within this chapter, we are not really treating minor day-to-day complaints of employees; these are usually well handled by managers and employees. If the manager fails to adequately deal with such complaints, they may well become grievances. However, our main focus will be on the more serious employee grievances that are not always handled in an effective manner.

Ownership of Employee Grievances

The level of employee grievances in any unit of an organisation is a very good barometer of the state of relationships between the immediate management team and those within the unit. Managers should give great attention to grievances so as to ensure that individuals are listened to and grievances are addressed in as positive a manner as the circumstances allow; this approach ensures that the overall set of relationships within the unit is optimised.

Managers and team leaders should see employee grievances in much the same way as customer complaints can be seen, as an opportunity to:

→ Understand the employee better

→ Become more familiar with the efforts of the employee

in trying to get to his/her grievance resolved

→ Be the deliverer of the 'result' within their own area/department rather than having results delivered from elsewhere

So, managers should try to look at grievances as their own property, their opportunity to work hard on resolution.

Grievances are Felt More in the 'Gut' than in the 'Head'

Most employees, when asked how they feel about a particular grievance, use emotive works such as 'demotivated', 'frustrated', 'turned-off', 'organisation does not care', 'treated unfairly' etc. The use of such phrases indicates clearly that many grievances are felt more in the gut than in the head. Very often, however, management's response systems are aimed at the head rather than taking due account of the level of emotion in the situation.

Most employees, when asked how they feel about a particular grievance, use emotive works such as 'demotivated', 'frustrated', 'turned-off', 'organisation does not care', 'treated unfairly' etc.

Panel 6.1

Best Practice Grievance Behaviour

→ Listen to the aggrieved employee

→ Check your understanding of their position

→ Adjourn, giving a time commitment for getting back to employee

→ Check out the issues with colleagues and/or HR

→ Return to employee with organisational resolution

Resolve Grievances at Lowest Level Possible

The first principle regarding the management of grievances is that they should be resolved at as low a level as possible in the organisation. Therefore, middle and senior management should strive to empower those at lower levels of management to be fully equipped with the knowledge and skills to effect a speedy resolution of employee grievances. Putting time and effort into such good people management will mean that employees will not feel the need to go higher in the organisation to have their grievances heard or resolved.

It is much more preferable for organisations to have grievances resolved at as low a level as possible otherwise the employee, as shown in Panel 6.2 below, will continue to go above front line management in the hope of getting a more favourable result.

Panel 6.2

Learning by Results

→ People in organisations quickly learn what behaviours pay off

→ They also learn through the results achieved by others

→ Just like the child at the supermarket who cries and gets sweets, they know what worked last time

→ If employees get speedier results at lower levels then there is an incentive for them to go for results at the same level again

→ Senior management should thus strive for a culture where results are achieved in respect of employee grievances at as low a level as possible

Resolve Grievances as Speedily as Possible

The second basic principle in respect of grievance resolution is that grievances should be resolved as speedily as possible and not placed on the long finger causing frustration to build on the part of the aggrieved employee. Therefore, managers should take all grievances seriously and try to resolve them in a relatively expeditious manner. In addition, if managers are unable to resolve the grievance within the timeframe that they indicated, then they should return to the aggrieved employees and inform them of the delay and give them a new commitment date.

In respect of timeframes for resolution, many organisations include within their Grievance Procedure the practice that managers at each level of the procedure have a certain number of days (usually 3 or 5) to resolve the grievance. Failure to do so or to get back to the aggrieved employee within that time can then lead to a second grievance – that of the procedure not being adhered to.

Grievance Structures and Processes

Most organisations have devised effective grievance procedures in line with best practice but managers frequently do not actually follow the procedure that is in place. A typical procedure is shown in Panel 6.3 below.

Panel 6.3

In-house Grievance Resolution Procedure – Best Practice

	Preferred Resolution Route	Alternative Route
Stage 1	Aggrieved employee is encouraged to take grievance up with their team leader	Employee sometimes encouraged to take their grievance up with their local Trade Union Representative
Stage 2	Failing resolution, the employee is encouraged to approach their manager at the level above team leader	Failing resolution at this stage employees are often encouraged to take the case to their Shop Steward
Stage 3	Failing resolution, the employee is encouraged to approach the next level Manager or Chief Executive	Failing resolution in-house the employee has the opportunity of taking their grievance to the full-time Trade Union Official

So, in the first instance, grievances should be resolved within the lowest box level, if at all possible. Within Stage 1 of the preferred resolution route is contained the primary work relationship (that is the relationship between team leader and team member) and the manager should be doing everything possible to build up that primary work relationship. With particular reference to grievance resolution, we should be empowering such team leaders with the knowledge, skill and freedom to treat grievances as comprehensively as shown throughout this chapter.

Consistency of Approach is Critical

As in so many other facets of management, consistency of approach across the organisation is important. Most managers in organisations might well resolve grievances along the lines indicated within this chapter but one could have two or three other managers in the organisation that are quite tardy in their approach. Such situations can give rise to the possibility of a bad atmosphere across the whole organisation.

Proactive Approaches to Grievance Resolution

As a final word on grievances, we should add that all line managers should be encouraged to stay very close to their staff as a matter of course. Being in such close relationship may provide them with the opportunity of proactive grievance resolution. It enables managers to anticipate grievances almost before the employees realise they have a grievance.

Summary of Chapter 6

→ Every manager/team leader should take an active interest in and full ownership of employee grievances

→ Our responses to grievances should take account of most employees being emotional about their personal grievances

→ Grievance should be resolved at as low a level as possible and in as speedy a manner as possible

→ Learning through results achieved is a powerful method – use it to advantage in grievance resolution!

→ All organisations should have a robust grievance procedure and a way of managing with consistency across the organisation

→ Managers/team leaders should strive to be proactive in grievance resolution – by beating the employee to their own grievance!

Handling Discipline

7

Chapter outline

→ Confront Disciplinary Issues Early
→ Pre-discipline Process
→ Consistency of Approach
→ Red Hot Stove
→ Progressive Disciplinary Process
→ Disciplinary Procedure
→ Gross Misconduct
→ Dismissal Process
→ Investigation Process
→ Disciplinary Hearing Prior to Dismissal
→ Principles of Natural Justice

Managers should try to get the best out of their staff by using good management practices such as coaching and performance management techniques. Discipline should be used to deal with poor performance and unacceptable work behaviours only when employees do not respond to good management. A central point is that managers must consider not only the content of the offence but make sure than they follow the correct process. Otherwise the disciplinary process may be deemed to be invalid.

For the most part, in this chapter we will deal with progressive discipline, which is used where there are repeated 'offences' by the same individual over time. The chapter refers briefly to more serious discipline situations that warrant the immediate consideration of dismissal, usually where gross misconduct has occurred.

Confront Disciplinary Issues Early

Line managers must confront any deviations from expected behaviour or job performance as early as possible. Failure to do so could result in:

- rewarding the deviant behaviour by not taking the offender to task

- such behaviour becoming the norm for that individual

- other employees becoming affected by the behaviour

with resulting reduced performance/poor behaviour

- other employees becoming disenchanted and/or de-motivated when they see no action being taken against a poor performer

Pre-discipline Process

Prior to contemplating progressive discipline for any employee, the competent manager will hold informal counselling discussions with the employee where they will:

- identify the deviation from required behaviour/ performance

- re-clarify expectations

- set review period and put necessary support in place for improved behaviour/ performance

- provide feedback and counselling

- explain the consequences of failure to improve

The above process is just good management embodying those elements of performance management that have been already treated within Chapter 6; it is also a necessary **pre-discipline process** and managers in organisations are well advised to ensure that they complete the above prior to entering a formal disciplinary process. In addition, managers must ensure that all employees are treated **equally and with fairness.**

Consistency of Approach

It is beneficial in disciplinary situations to review how other employees have been treated in similar situations. There are serious difficulties in proceeding against an employee in respect of an offence for which other employees have not been disciplined. These difficulties may be lessened if you have clearly announced in advance a change in response to certain behaviours, such as a change in absenteeism rules and procedures. Failure to treat employees equally leaves the manager open to a charge of victimisation which might be difficult to defend. Try to follow the Red Hot Stove Rule in Panel 7.1.

Panel 7.1

Red Hot Stove Rule

The Red Hot Stove provides an excellent guide for managers in disciplinary matters:

→ **Warning:** because the stove is red hot, it provides a fair warning that there are serious consequences for touching it

→ **Immediate:** as soon as it is touched, it burns

→ **Consistent:** every time it is touched, it burns

Panel 7.1 (contd)

→ **Impersonal:** it makes no difference who touches it

It works. People do not touch red hot stoves.

Progressive Disciplinary Process

This process is so called because of the progressive nature of the action taken. It is usually used to address work performance issues such as:

→ poor quality or quantity of work

→ carelessness

→ failing to follow operating procedures

It is also used to deal with unacceptable work behaviours in relation to:

→ time-keeping

→ attendance

→ house-keeping

→ HR policies

Good managers know that they must follow an appropriate disciplinary process such as the one set out in Panel 7.2 opposite.

Panel 7.2

A Good Discriplinary Process

→ Complete pre-discipline approach including re-clarification of expectations and feedback

→ Identify issues with employee and seek their input/explanations

→ If performance/behaviour is still unsatisfactory, say so and put in place sanctions at appropriate level depending on the stage of the procedure at which action is being taken

→ Agree specific ways of improving performance/ behaviour

→ Provide support required for improvement

→ Review progress within a specific timeframe

Disciplinary Procedure

The process described within Panel 7.2 should be a manager's natural way of behaviour when confronted by disciplinary situations. It should be used at all stages in the progressive disciplinary procedure that exists within most organisations. See example of such a procedure within Panel 7.3 below.

Panel 7.3

Disciplinary Procedure

→ Counselling Discussion

- Informal but requires record to be kept

→ Verbal Warning

- Informal but requires record to be kept

→ Written Warning

- Formal and requiring a full investigation

→ Final Written Warning

- Formal and requiring a full investigation

→ Suspension, pending Investigation

- Usually just a holding position whilst arranging an investigation

→ Dismissal

- Formal and requiring a full investigation

Some progressive discipline procedures require managers to move through each of the above stages for each category of offence; thus one may have an employee at a verbal warning stage vis-à-vis their attendance when a job performance issue arises that may have them at the counselling stage.

Managers who have to deal with progressive discipline should realise that the best chance of changing behaviour is at the informal stages (counselling and verbal warning). At each of these stages, they have the opportunity to work directly with the employee and perhaps have more influence on them. As the procedure escalates to the more formal levels the meetings can become more defensive and argumentative with the consequence that it is more difficult to change behaviour.

> Managers who have to deal with progressive discipline should realise that the best chance of changing behaviour is at the informal stages (counselling and verbal warning).

Although the majority of progressive disciplinary processes commence at the counselling stage or verbal warning stage, it is possible, for more serious offences, to commence the process at written warning or at final written warning stage. Where there is a failure to improve at a particular stage, the disciplinary process escalates up to a stage when a decision to dismiss the employee must be considered. In the case of gross misconduct, the disciplinary process commences at the final stage.

Gross Misconduct

Gross Misconduct refers to offences which automatically proceed directly to Final Written Warning or Dismissal depending on the gravity of the situation. Most organisations will specify what they regard as situations that could be seen as Gross Misconduct, such as those listed in Panel 7.4 below.

Panel 7.4

Examples of Gross Misconduct – not an Exhaustive List

→ Theft/fraud

→ Violent conduct

→ Wilful damage to company property

→ Bullying/Harassment/ Sexual Harassment of a fellow employee, customer, supplier or member of the public

Panel 7.4 (contd)

→ Misuse of the Internet or e-mail, particularly downloading and disseminating pornographic material

→ Dealing with fellow employees, customers, suppliers or members of the public in a manner that clearly contravenes company values

→ Refusal to carry out reasonable instructions

→ Compromising the viability of the organisation

→ Breach of some fundamental term of the employment contract

Dismissal Process

Dismissal is a very serious disciplinary step and every precaution should be taken to ensure that the rights of the employee are not violated and that the organisation is not left open to a charge of unfair or wrongful dismissal. There are four questions that need to be considered to ensure that justice is not only done, but is seen to be done.

❶ Is the process taking place at the right stage of the procedure?

❷ Has there been a full and proper investigation?

❸ Have the principles of natural justice been followed?

❹ Has due process been observed throughout?

Investigation Process

Before proceeding to a disciplinary interview which might lead to a dismissal, it is necessary to conduct a thorough investigation of the circumstances leading up to a decision to consider disciplinary action. This investigation should be conducted by an independent person and is usually done by another manager who is a peer to the manager taking the disciplinary action. Usually it takes a number of days to complete the investigation and the decision may be made to suspend the employee on pay until a decision is made. They receive full pay to demonstrate that no view has been taken regarding the outcome of the investigation. Often the employee will be interviewed as part of the investigation and/ or will be given an opportunity to comment on the investigator's report. If the investigator's report finds that the employee has a case to answer, then he or she will be called to a disciplinary hearing.

Disciplinary Hearing Prior to Dismissal

This disciplinary hearing must consider two factors: content and process. Content refers to the substance of the charge. It will be repeated offences in the case of progressive discipline or it may relate to gross misconduct. Process relates to ensuring that the organisation's disciplinary procedure is properly followed and the principles of natural justice set out in Panel 7.5 are adhered to.

It is particularly important to afford employees their full Rights of Natural Justice when serious disciplinary action is being considered. Many cases of Gross Misconduct that appear 'cut and dried' fail on a technicality such as the relevant Manager being too hasty, and not fully hearing the employee's response and/or affording representation rights to the employee.

Many organisations take Gross Misconduct sufficiently seriously that they escalate such issues to be dealt with by higher levels of Management and/or to HR.

Panel 7.5
Principles of Natural Justice

Right	Words used to ensure Right is afforded to employee
To know the Offence	"We need to talk about ....., which could be a disciplinary matter"
Right of Reply	"I need to hear what you have to say about this"
Right to a Fair Hearing	"We will make sure that this hearing is conducted in a way that is fair to all parties"
Right of Representation	"..... and I need to hear what your representative has to say on your behalf"
Separate prosecutor and judge	"We must make sure that the person hearing the case is not involved in it in any other way
Right to Due Consideration	"Now that I have conducted the hearing, I need to take time to consider all of the issues ....."
Penalty fit the Crime	"I will impose a penalty that is proportionate to the offence that was carried out given the overall circumstances of the case."

Discipline should only be used as an instrument of last resort. It has serious repercussions for the employee and, carried out in an inappropriate manner, it can have significant employee relations and legal implications for the manager.

→ Gross Misconduct must be managed very delicately and one must fully ensure that all processes and procedures are to the level of Best Practice when affording the employee their Rights of Natural Justice.

Summary of Chapter 7

→ Managers must confront incidents of ill discipline - performance and/or behaviour issues as early as possible

→ Before commencing discipline managers must engage in pre-discipline —re-clarify expectations, monitor performance and provide support/feedback

→ Disciplinary issues that are not confronted reward the individual and will encourage similar poor performance behaviour in others

→ A good disciplinary process should spur managers to move towards sanctions that fit the situation and provide support/ review thereafter

→ It is best to work hard at the informal level of a Disciplinary Procedure — that is your best chance of changing behaviour

→ The Rights of Natural Justice must be afforded to all employees in disciplinary situations- see Panel 7.5

→ Investigations should be fair and clearly seen to be so

8 Learning and Development

Chapter outline

→ Competencies Explained
→ Promoting Learning and Development
→ Taking a Learner's Viewpoint
→ Getting the Best From Off-the-Job Training

Developing the performance of team members is a central theme of this book. This chapter deals with one of the most important ways in which managers can improve performance, i.e. by developing the capability of team members. Whilst it is not necessary or always possible for managers to create a team of world beaters, their objective should be to develop team members so that they can perform at their personal best.

Teams which focus on development as a value, not only perform better, they also attract talented people to their ranks. Individual employees nowadays look for a life-long learning approach to their work and careers. They want to work for managers who share that value.

This chapter explores a number of key facets of learning and development at the team level and provides practical tools which managers can use to develop the capabilities of team members. It starts with competencies which are the building blocks of learning and development.

Competencies Explained

The idea of competencies was introduced in Chapter 2 of this book when looking at how to recruit staff. Selecting people for a position is the easiest way to consider competencies. Do managers want to hire people who have qualifications or do they want people who have the knowledge, skills and attitudes required to do a job? In an ideal world, the new hire would have both but if a manager had to make a choice, then competence is a better guide to future performance than qualifications.

Panel 8.1

Competency Framework

A competency framework breaks down the areas of capability under a number of different headings. These headings can in turn be further broken down to more specific areas.

The examples given below are intended as illustrative of the more widely accepted competencies. They do not always adhere to strict academic definitions of competencies.

→ **Personal:** personal effectiveness; interpersonal skills; character (personality and values); disposition (inclination to perform)

→ **Technical:** level of expertise; qualifications; licenses; Continuing Professional Development (CPD)

→ **Managerial:** leadership; planning; execution;

Panel 8.1 (contd)

problem-solving and decision-making; strategy development and team-leadership

→ **Business:** business acumen; functional (marketing; finance; sales; operations, HR etc) know-how; risk management

The level of competency required should be assessed for each position. For example, a manager could use a scale such as a) awareness; b) general understanding; c) professional knowledge; and d) expert.

Using a competency framework enables managers to break down the competencies required for any position. It has been very well established that increasing individual or team competency has a consequent increase in confidence, albeit within the sphere of that particular competence. However, of great importance for line managers, is the fact that if one further develops different competencies, the cumulative effect goes beyond just an increase in confidence to an increase in self-esteem.

Promoting Learning and Development

There are four roles which a manager can play in promoting learning and development in their teams.

❶ As an **Instructor,** the manager is directly involved in teaching a team member a new competence.

❷ As a **Coach,** very often with a performance focus, the manager becomes directly involved with the team member in trying to develop his/her competencies. The key behaviours of the manager as a coach are: analysing performance, giving feedback to the team member, reviewing options for improvement and finally, action-planning.

❸ As a **Mentor**, the manager explains the wider context, provides a sounding board for ideas, challenges pre-conceptions and finally he or she reviews outcomes with team members.

❹ Finally, as a **Facilitator**, in a range of different ways, the manager provides opportunities and resources to team members to pursue their development.

Managers, who recognise that they achieve results through the work of others, are prepared to devote time, to a greater or lesser extent, to fulfil one or more of these roles with each of their team members.

Taking a Learner's Viewpoint

When managers are creating a learning culture, one of the values they must instil is that individual team members should take shared responsibility for their own development. Once they have done so, then the manager can provide valuable assistance by acting in one of the roles described above. A manager must recognise that individual team members have different learning styles. Some team members can readily assimilate learning from a book while others prefer a more action oriented 'learning by doing' approach. Various authorities have identified four different learning styles as described in Panel 8.2. A review of different learning styles reveals a wide range of training and development options available to a manager.

Panel 8.2

Matching Learning Styles and Methods

Below are the four main learning styles that individuals display together with examples of different learning activities associated with each.

Doer: Doers refer to the 'school of hard knocks' as being the best way to learn. They rely on work experience for their development. Nowadays elearning approaches can be used to facilitate just-in-time training for Doers who get training/new information as they require it.

Current role/promotions/ transfers/secondments/ work assignments/exchange programmes/acting up/job rotation

Reflector: Reflectors take time out to learn from experience. They benefit from coaching and performance reviews in which the lessons from today form the basis for a new way of doing things in the future.

Coaching/mentoring/performance reviews/360 degree feedback/ assessment centres

Theorist: Theorists have a tendency to separate learning from the working environment. They rely on off-the-job training like courses and books for enhancing their competencies. They are at an advantage when there is a need for new ways of thinking about how things are done.

Training courses/books/seminars/ centres of excellence visits/ benchmarking/elearning

Explorer: Explorers like to learn by trial and error. Their approach is similar to Doers other than that they focus on trial and error in new areas.

Task forces/skunk works/project teams/change programmes

Each of the four learning styles has its advantages and disadvantages. A balanced approach to development is probably the best and managers should encourage their team members to try out different learning styles. There is an increasing tendency to use 'blended learning' approaches in recognition that there is no one best style and that a combination of learning styles has the most impact.

Getting the Best From Off-the-Job Training

There are many situations when attending off-the-job training seems to provide the best opportunity for team members to develop new know-how and skills. Yet too often the results are disappointing with no discernible performance improvement after training. There are many considerations which a manager should take into account in order to enhance the benefits of off-the-job training for team members, such as:

❶ **Behaviourally stated learning objectives** (BSLOs): the vast majority of training programmes are enhanced by the preparation of behaviourally stated learning objectives for each competence area. BSLOs express in behavioural terms what the learner will be able to do after the training programme, to what standard and in what conditions. The following is an example of a BSLO: "Participants on this programme will be able to develop an annual budget for their work unit based on company standards without any assistance from the Finance Department."

❷ **Matching the objectives with the methodology:** managers who are reviewing a proposal for off-the-job training need to examine whether the BSLOs are achievable in the timescales involved and the training methodologies proposed. The principles of aviation can be learned from text book in less than an hour. Learning to fly a light airplane will take a good deal longer and cannot be achieved in a classroom although it may be done in a simulator.

❸ **Transfer of learning:** no matter how good the programme is, transfer of learning from the classroom to the workplace will not take place unless the conditions are right to make it happen. These conditions may include time to practice new skills on the job, the facilities required and the support of colleagues. Clearly the manager plays a critical role in providing the right environment for a transfer of learning to take place. The two most important things which a manager should do are to hold pre and post training discussions with participants undertaking the training. The first discussion is concerned with setting the context for the training and for managing expectations in relation to the training. The second discussion is concerned with understanding what has been learned and seeing how it can be applied in the workplace. Both discussions also serve to demonstrate the manager's commitment to the learning process.

❹ **Programme evaluation:** the most accepted ways to evaluate training programmes have been defined by Donald Kirkpatrick (1994). He identified four main methods as follows:

a. **Reaction:** how participants feel about the training event

b. **Learning:** what people learned at the event

c. **Behaviours:** whether people behaved differently following the training

d. **Results:** whether performance improved as a result of the training.

By focusing on these four considerations, managers can make a significant contribution to the effectiveness of off-the-job training initiatives in their work units.

This chapter highlighted the manager's role in learning and development and its importance to the organisation and to its people. It looked at the range of learning and development initiatives from an individual's perspective and showed how managers can get more 'bang for their buck' from off-the-job training.

Summary of Chapter 8

→ Managers should be committed to learning and development because of the impact on work unit performance and team member satisfaction

→ Competencies are the building blocks of training and development processes

→ Managers, through four different roles that they can play, have a central role in promoting learning and development:

- Instructor

- Coach

- Mentor

- Facilitator

→ It is possible to identify a whole array of learning and development opportunities by taking a learner's viewpoint into account, particularly the four different learning styles:

- Doer

- Reflector

- Theorist

- Explorer

→ By focusing on four different areas, managers can ensure a valuable return from off-the-job training initiatives:

- Behaviourally stated learning objectives

- Matching the objectives with the methodology

- Transfer of learning

- Programme evaluation.

9

Upholding Dignity and Respect in the Workplace

Chapter outline

→ What is Covered
→ Role of the Manager
→ Responding to a Complaint
→ Managing the Process
  - Hearing the Complaint
  - Responding to the Complaint
    - Informal Process
  - Responding to the Complaint
    - Formal Process
  - Follow-up

Every manager has a responsibility to uphold the right of all employees to be treated with dignity and respect. They must ensure that all staff, particularly those in leadership positions, behave in ways that are consistent with this objective. When managers do not uphold the right of employees, performance declines and employees suffer needless stress. In addition, the manager and the organisation may become liable in law as a result of a failure to act appropriately.

The right of employees to be treated with dignity and respect is often set out in what is sometimes called a 'Dignity at Work' Policy. The objective of this policy is to promote a working environment in which employees are able to work to the best of their abilities without being undermined by others. Usually in organisations, breaches of this policy leave the perpetrator liable to disciplinary action.

This chapter defines the behaviours that are usually covered by Dignity at Work Policies. It also outlines the role of the manager in upholding the policy and the actions which a manager should take to respond to complaints under the policy.

What is Covered

Dignity at Work Policies usually cover three areas: Bullying, Harassment and Sexual Harassment, whether carried out by a member(s) of staff, a customer, a client or a business contact of the employer; the policy applies to work on the employer's premises, assignments off those premises and at social occasions that are work related. Different organisations and legal codes define each of these areas in different ways. However, at a general level, they may be defined as follows:

❶ **Bullying** is repeated inappropriate behaviour – verbal, physical or psychological – which has the effect of undermining an individual's right to dignity and respect at work.

❷ **Harassment** is inappropriate behaviour which is aimed at a person because of some characteristic which is covered by law such as race, age, religion, sexual orientation etc.

❸ **Sexual harassment** relates to inappropriate behaviour based on a person's gender which has the effect of undermining that person's right to respect and dignity. It may include inappropriate comments, jokes, touching, posting of pornographic materials and requests for sexual favours in addition to the behaviours described above.

Generally speaking, in relation to each of the three complaints, it is the employee who determines whether the behaviour is inappropriate. The employee is also entitled to change his or her mind about whether certain behaviours are acceptable.

On the other hand, a complaint under one of the above headings will fail, if the behaviour arose simply from the exercise of legitimate management action, e.g. in dealing with poor performance or work-related behaviours.

Role of the Manager

Managers need to be proactive in promoting a culture of dignity and respect in the workplace. Otherwise when an incident arises, they may be found culpable for allowing a situation to arise which endangered the health and safety of their staff and/or they were in breach of legal obligations. The responsibilities of managers in this regard are set out in Panel 9.1.

Panel 9.1

Responsibilities of Managers

→ Managers should know the company's policy and have the skills to implement it

→ They should not engage in any of the three categories of behaviour concerned

→ They should communicate the importance of the policy to all staff at induction and during the

---

Panel 9.1 (contd)

---

on-going management of their work units

→ Managers should be alert to any incidents that may be occurring

→ They should respond immediately and appropriately as soon as they become aware of a problem and to any complaint made to them.

Responding to a Complaint

It is an unfortunate fact of organisational life that almost all managers will have to deal with a complaint regarding a dignity at work issue at some time or another. Their own proactive behaviour will determine the frequency of such events and the quality of their response to incidents will determine the extent of the adverse consequences that arise from them. Panel 9.2 sets out guiding principles for managers responding to complaints under Dignity at Work Policies.

Managers need to be proactive in promoting a culture of dignity and respect in the workplace.

Panel 9.2

Responding to Complaints — Guiding Principles

→ The most important guiding principle for managers is to take all complaints seriously. It is far easier to nip a problem in the bud than to deal with the complexity of human emotions and conflicting evidence after a problem escalates.

→ The rights of both parties, alleged victim and alleged perpetrator, need to be respected throughout.

→ The processes, both informal and formal, need to be conducted throughout with strict confidentiality.

→ Both parties to the complaint should be provided with the appropriate level of support, in the form of expertise or counselling, to help them through the complaint resolution process.

→ Managers will find that strict adherence to the organisation policy is usually the best approach.

→ Justice delayed is justice denied — cases should be dealt with speedily for the benefit of both parties.

→ Although an informal process works best when no notes are taken during the meeting, you should ensure that a written record is prepared immediately after the meeting.

A manager should note that all complaints are formal even though it may be decided to respond 'informally'. Once a manager is aware of a problem, then he or she is required to ensure that it is fully resolved.

Managing the Process

There are four main steps in managing the resolution process:

❶ Hearing the complaint

❷ Responding to the complaint - informal process

❸ Responding to the complaint - formal process

❹ Follow-up

Each of these steps is dealt with below.

1. Hearing the Complaint

Usually a complaint is made verbally to a manager or is referred to the manager by another person.

The manager should meet with the alleged victim to discuss the nature of the complaint. Managers must be conscious of employee sensitivities when they find themselves handling complaints of Bullying, Harassment and/ or Sexual Harassment. Such situations are usually very traumatic for all concerned and it is important that managers behave in keeping with best practice, as shown in Panel 9.3 below.

Panel 9.3

Hearing a Complaint

→ Listen with empathy.

→ Keep the discussion as informal as possible.

→ Try to obtain a full and accurate outline of the nature of the complaint including circumstances, witnesses and dates.

→ Generally take no notes during the discussion but ensure that you write up a record of the discussion immediately after the meeting.

→ Review whether the matter is an appropriate issue for the Dignity at Work Policy or should be dealt with in some other way, such as through the Grievance Procedure. Take advice from your HR Advisor or your manager regarding such a decision.

→ Discuss the Dignity at Work Policy with the individual.

→ Advise the person that the alleged perpetrator must be informed of the complaint and that this is best done by the complainant if at all possible.

→ Review the options that are available to the alleged victim. These include dealing with the matter informally or formally under the policy.

→ Review whether it is necessary to take protective action such as separating the parties if they work together. In such a case, it will normally be the alleged perpetrator who is moved.

→ Agree an action plan and a follow-up date.

→ Write up a full account of the meeting — this note is for the record only and should not at this stage be shared with the complainant or alleged perpetrator.

2. Responding to the Complaint — Informal Process

Ideally, the manager will be able to keep the process for handling the complaint as informal as possible. It is important for us to stress that this approach provides the best chance of maintaining working relationships in the future. As soon as one moves to the more formal stage of statements being put in writing and passed to both parties, then the situation becomes much more intractable.

There are three forms of informal response:

→ In the first instance, the **alleged victim undertakes to raise the complaint** with the alleged perpetrator saying what the problem is and how they would like things to be in the future. In this case, the manager's role is to empower the individual to address his/her concerns directly to the alleged perpetrator and provide coaching and support for this dialogue. This approach is the preferred option and works well in most cases.

→ The complainant may be reluctant or feel unable to confront the perpetrator, in which case, **the manager can undertake to speak directly with the alleged perpetrator.** The objective of this discussion is to reach agreement with regard to incidents and how they impacted on the complainant. It may be necessary to point out the consequences for the perpetrator of a continuation of the behaviours in question. The objective is to reach a mutually satisfactory agreement regarding future behaviours. In this situation the manager handling the complaint is carrying out the role of an informal mediator.

→ The third informal approach is **to engage the help of an experienced mediator.** Many organisations have arrangements in place for the selection of a mediator from an internal panel of trained mediators. If such do not exist, then an external, experienced mediator should be engaged. The mediator works with the parties to reach common ground with regard to understanding the nature of the behaviours complained of and their impact on the complainant. Resolution normally includes a commitment regarding future behaviour and a mechanism to deal with problems that may arise.

A number of benefits ensue when the manager empowers the individual to approach the alleged perpetrator and state how they feel about the behaviour of the other. Not alone is it an important step on the path to resolution, but it may be valuable to the complainant to feel that they have 'confronted' the alleged perpetrator and asserted their view. Doing so will be of great assistance in their 'moving on' once the situation has been resolved. The key behaviours involved in helping the complainant through such a conversation are outlined within Panel 9.4 below.

Panel 9.4

Ways of Helping the Complainant to Talk Directly with the Alleged Perpetrator

---

→ Explain that taking an informal approach is decidedly the best option for resolution.

→ Influence the individual so that they realise that they are likely to get to a better place personally if they, themselves, address their concerns directly to the alleged perpetrator.

→ Explain the support or skill development that the individual will receive to help prepare for the dialogue with the alleged perpetrator.

→ Highlight some of the more difficult aspects of following the formal procedure towards a resolution of the complaint.

→ Explore whether or not there is another trusted person on whom the complainant can rely for support.

→ Ask the complainant to let you know whether or not the conversation with the alleged perpetrator resolved the issue. Confirm that you will be prepared to take follow-up action if the conversation with the alleged perpetrator fails to have the desired result.

As the individuals involved in situations such as these commence talking about their differences, they should focus as early as possible on the way forward rather than the past. Thus it is useful for such individuals to work toward some values about how they will relate to one another in the future, and particularly on some of the behaviours that would give expression to those values.

Examples of matching values and behaviours are set in Panel 9.5.

Panel 9.5

Values and Behaviours - Examples

Values	Behaviours
Dignity and respect	Will address each other directly, but in a calm respectful manner, both in private and in public.
Support and Review	Will provide support to one another on day-to-day issues and will always review work directly with one another in the first instance.
Allocation of credit for work	Will give direct and indirect credit for work done to the party that has undertaken the work.
Teamwork	Will provide all necessary collaboration, information and feedback to facilitate optimum team performance.
Diversity	Will respect each other's right to be different individually and together seek to find synergies in that difference to enhance a better performance and harmony in the relationship.

As mentioned above, in an ideal world, complaints in respect of dignity at work issues would be dealt with informally. Unfortunately, this approach is not always possible and it may be necessary to follow a formal process to resolve the complaint.

3. Responding to the Complaint - Formal Process

A formal approach to the resolution of a complaint is required in a minority of cases such as:

→ When the alleged perpetrator denies that the behaviours complained of occurred or constituted a breach of a Dignity at Work Policy

→ When the complainant does not feel able to confront the alleged perpetrator

→ Where the alleged perpetrator continues with the inappropriate action after an informal intervention

→ Where the issue is so serious that it warrants formal action and may result in disciplinary action being taken.

Failure to resolve the complaint either informally or through mediation pushes one towards a Formal Investigation and this approach is usually outside the remit of the local manager. The issue would then be deemed to be sufficiently serious that it should be passed to more senior levels of management who will initiate a formal quasi-legal investigation in accordance with the provisions of the policy.

4. Follow-up

In all cases, whether dealt with informally or formally, a manager must ensure that the terms of the resolution of the complaint have been observed by both parties. The manager should follow-up to ensure that there are no further problems. He or she must be vigilant in ensuring that there is no '**victimisation**' of the complainant, i.e. that there have been no negative consequences for the complainant as a result of bringing a complaint under the Dignity at Work Policy.

Summary of Chapter 9

→ Every employee has a right to dignity and respect at work

→ Managers should work hard at creating and sustaining a culture of dignity and respect within the workplace

> If confronted with Bullying or Harassment situations the manager should:

- Listen with empathy

- Work in a solution-oriented mode

- Maintain total confidentiality

→ The process of resolution should be kept as informal as possible

→ The rights of both parties should be respected throughout

→ Where possible the complainant should be empowered to talk directly with the perpetrator

→ Mediation should be tried if the above informal resolution efforts fail

→ Failure to resolve the complaint informally or through mediation, may result in the more difficult route of formal investigation taking place.

10 Change Management

Chapter outline

→ Inevitability of Change
→ Identifying Future Direction of Organisational Change
→ Key Approaches to Change
→ Readiness for Change
→ Resistance to Change
→ Communication
→ People and Change
→ Change Processes
→ Transformational Leadership

Inevitability of Change

Change is ever present all around us, particularly within organisational life. The rate and pace of change are sometimes mind boggling. It is here to stay and managers require Change Management Skills as one of their key competencies.

One of the key issues facing line managers is the organisation's readiness for change at any particular time.

Identifying Future Direction of Organisational Change

Managers play a significant role in anticipating the future direction of change that is pertinent to the organisation or to their own unit/section/department. Not alone should these managers anticipate such change but they must go beyond to the point of shaping how the unit/section/department can respond to the upcoming changes.

Coping with change will be all the more effective if it is built on advance views of where the principal changes will be and agreement on planning how such changes will be brought about.

Key Approaches to Change

There may well be occasions when it is appropriate for 'a big bang' approach to change (otherwise known as frame-breaking change) being taken in organisations. However, managers can have a much better chance of achieving buy-in from those principally involved when, if time permits, a more incremental approach is taken. From as early as possible, the planning process should involve those most affected.

Readiness for Change

One of the key issues facing line managers is the organisation's readiness for change at any particular time. This idea of readiness implies that the organisation may not be fully 'ready' for whatever is proposed. Being unready may arise for a variety of reasons such as dated technology, inadequate resources or resistance from key individuals/teams. So it may be that the manager has to spend some time preparing people in organisations for upcoming change and helping them to understand the need for change.

Resistance to Change

It is a feature of our human condition that oftentimes our first response to a major change is one of denial and resistance. Organisations can reduce the level of resistance for a particular change if they have worked in the past towards bringing people through small steps of change, sometimes even in situations where the change is not actually necessary. This process brings about a situation where individuals get comfortable with moving from one task or one process to another with ease; they therefore are at a better stage of readiness when a major change emerges. Some alternative ways in which one could breakdown resistance to change is shown in Panel 10.1.

Panel 10.1

Some Ways of Overcoming Resistance to Change

→ Communicate full picture early on in the change process

→ Listen carefully to individuals/team concerns

→ Show clearly the consequences of not changing

→ Help individuals/teams to see the 'imperative' of moving with change

→ Paint positive/realistic picture of life after change

→ Help individuals construct change imperatives for themselves and others

Communication

The requirement for good communication mentioned above is not a once-off obligation; it is an on-going process where optimum communication is provided to all individuals and teams — communication that takes account of their perspective and needs. There is often a need to allow sufficient time after a communication process to permit team members become accustomed to the proposed change.

There is often a need to ensure also that the communication stresses that the change will in fact happen and that the consultation process is more about the 'how' than about whether or not change will occur.

People and Change

Some individuals and/or organisations see change as a technical, structural or a systems process. It is however very much about people and all major change efforts should take account, from the outset, of this people dimension. Panel 10.2 overleaf puts forward some key issues regarding People and Change.

Panel 10.2

People and Change

→ All significant change involves people

→ People can have their own reasons for resistance; we need to help them to overcome these hurdles

→ Oftentimes staff resistance is based on lack of information and/or mistrust of management

→ People may not see a clear new role after change – they need help with this concern

→ Staff need bridges built for them that will lead them towards change in easy steps.

Several of the techniques referred to in the previous Chapter on Learning and Development, which bring about a continuous learning organisation, are extremely relevant to establishing a healthy climate for change within organisations.

Change Processes

All managers need to experiment with change processes so that they develop the requisite skills for effecting meaningful change.

Such a step-by-step process is contained within Panel 10.3 below.

Panel 10.3

Suggested Change Processes

→ Clearly understand the rationale for the change and communicate same to all concerned

→ Take time to understand peoples fears and help them overcome their concerns

→ State clearly the objectives of the change and the planned stages within the change process

→ Establish milestones and, once the change consensus has been achieved, work hard at creating and sustaining momentum

→ Encourage and support staff who are particularly affected by the change

→ Conduct interim reviews of what is going well and what could be improved

→ Once the target of change is achieved, check that all elements are fully completed

→ De-brief the total experience with an eye to future learning.

Transformational Leadership

A final thought in respect of change management stems from the work on Transformational Leadership which requires leaders to move beyond transactional leadership ('do this for this reward'). Transformational leaders strive to see where the unit/section/department needs to be going in the future through visioning and other methods of 'painting pictures' of new realities. It is critically important, within this concept of transformational leadership, that such visualisation on a future position is carried out in an inclusive manner. In that way, it is possible to involve many team members. They can then work out the best means of moving towards this collective vision. See the note on Transformational Leader's Behaviour in Panel 10.4 below.

Panel 10.4

Transformational Leader's Behaviour

→ Increasing awareness within team members of task importance and value

→ Engaging team members in the process of inclusive visioning and selling/promoting that vision

→ Getting others to focus on team/organisational goals, rather than own interests

→ Evoking strong emotions and identification with the leader

→ Inspirationally motivating through individualised consideration

→ Embedding strong ethical values in the visioning and change programme

Each of the above team leader behaviours greatly facilitate the process of change.

Summary of Chapter 10

→ Change is now a constant —
we must skill ourselves to
manage it

→ Sometimes frame-breaking fast
change is appropriate, usually
where speed of response is of
the essence

→ Oftentimes a slower
incremental change process
may be used, usually where
time is not a constraint but
there is strong resistance

→ One may have to bring one's
unit/section/department to a
state of readiness for change

→ Resistance comes in many
forms - embrace it, understand
it and help staff deal with it

→ Communicate...
Communicate...Communicate

→ People are at the heart of
change, so be sure to involve
them as early as possible

→ The skills of Transformation
Leadership will greatly
strenghten your approach to
Change Management.

Enhancing Personal Commitment of Staff

11

Chapter outline

→ Utilising the Power and Skills in Others

→ Moving from Authoritarian to Facilitative Approaches

→ Acquiring Facilitation Skills

→ 'Letting-go' and Developing Confidence in Others

→ The Commitment Equation

→ Organisational Skills and Learning

Utilising the Power and Skills in Others

In recent years, many line managers have come to realise that employees have far more to give than the organisation allows them. This insight has led to the realisation that there are substantial benefits to be gained by unleashing the power and skill within others and bringing these newly released skills to bear on organisational life.

Moving from Authoritarian to Facilitative Approaches

The manager's mode of managing is key to unleashing this power. One usually cannot do so if trapped solely in an authoritarian mode of leadership. Thus it behoves all of us to have a range of Leadership Skills, and perhaps to move to more facilitative approaches.

Acquiring Facilitation Skills

The first step in acquiring facilitation skills is the realisation of the distinction between authoritative modes of leadership and more facilitative modes. In the authoritative mode one is more regularly seeing all of the relevant information as residing within oneself and therefore engaging in behaviours that really could be categorised as telling the other individual/team what is required. More facilitative approaches are built on the belief that much of the information required for the task resides within the individual/team.

Once this realisation is in place, managers need to realise that they can best develop their facilitative skills through practice. In real-life situations they should go out of their way to take aboard the view of individuals/teams and give them increasing responsibility for playing a more active role in the totality of the issues around the task they are completing.

Very often line managers gather information from team members and then apply problem solving and/or decision making techniques in respect of that information prior to passing the information back to the group as well as perhaps to others.

This scenario provides an opportunity for managers to develop their facilitation skills. They can allow individuals/teams to play a greater part in the problem solving and decision making processes, thereby building mutual confidence in one another around that particular task.

More facilitative approaches are built on the belief that much of the information required for the task resides within the individual/team.

Panel 11.1

Tips for Acquiring Facilitation Skills

→ Identify opportunities for some problem-solving/decision-making to be devolved to others

→ Coach those involved towards the skills required

→ Support 'from a distance', as required

→ Provide the 'enabling conditions' for success

→ Review with individuals/teams

→ Reward with another problem-solving/decision-making problem

The unleashing of these skills requires a significant move from old-style authoritarian type management and a move to more facilitative approaches. This approach in no way implies that line managers may not be required to utilise a direct style of management as some situations arise from time to time. However, there is decidedly a strong move towards line managers having within their repertoire of skills some more facilitative approaches than have been practised in the past. Utilisation of these skills delivers greater involvement of staff which in turn releases greater commitment to the goals of the organisation.

'Letting-go' and Developing Confidence in Others

One of the first difficulties that presents itself for managers who want to go on this journey is overcoming the personal obstacle of 'letting-go'. This really requires the local manager to identify things that he or she is doing that could be transferred to others and to then challenge themselves as to what they have to do to let go. It may be that they will be required to give the task to others in small bites so that they start to develop the confidence in that other person or team to be able to do that portion of the task prior to giving them more. This raises the critical issue of confidence which is required both in the person letting-go — that they have confidence in the other and within the other individual and/or team that they develop confidence from undertaking these tasks.

A further dimension of this 'letting-go' is that managers need to be able to measure the success of this approach. Measurement of success can be put in place as part of a performance management process. In turn, the manager can include quantitative measures of the value of this style of management in performance review disuccsions with his/her own manager.

> ## Panel 11.2
>
> # Tips for Letting-go
>
> ---
>
> → Convince yourself that taking opportunity to let go could be good for you and others
>
> → Find something small but meaningful to start the process with
>
> → Discuss the 'hows and wherefore' of the approach with the individual/team to help their confidence
>
> → Plan the steps you wish to take and go for it
>
> → Provide support but resist the temptation to jump in, unless in an emergency.

teams have as confidence and self-esteem rise and they attribute that to specific actions taken by line managers. Consequently they become more committed to the unit/section/department/organisation as a result.

> ## Panel 11.3
>
> # The Commitment Equation
>
> ---
>
> → An increase in personal/team competence = an increase in personal/team confidence
>
> → Further increase development by adding other competencies = an increase in personal/team esteem
>
> → Enhanced esteem delivers extra commitment and effort.

The Commitment Equation

In an earlier chapter we outlined the benefit of developing confidence within individuals and/or the team through adding further competencies to their existing range of competencies.

There is considerable evidence that additional personal/team commitment can be obtained by bringing an individual or team through the competence/confidence/self-esteem path. This commitment devolves from the good feelings that individuals/

Organisational Skills and Learning

The contribution of empowered team members becomes further increased through the development of the organisational networking skills of individuals/teams. Such skills are honed through sharing across departments, insights gained in the on-going search for greater effectiveness. The spirit of the various initiatives across

91

the organisation will enhance individual/team skills and also create great organisational learning.

Summary of Chapter 11

→ Search for ways of unleashing the power and skill within others

→ Develop further skills of a facilitative style of management by utilising the tips in Panel 11.1

→ Practice ways of 'letting go' some things that have been hitherto important to you – see tips within Panel 11.2

→ Search for opportunities to enhance the confidence and self-esteem of individuals/teams

→ When such opportunities are identified coach the individual/team along the competence/confidence/self esteem continuum

→ Extend through networking these skills across departments and through the whole organisation.

Positive Employee Relations

12

Chapter outline

→ Enlightened Leadership
→ Team Development through Empowerment
→ Team-based Performance Management
→ Proactive Attitudes and Behaviours

Positive employee relations is concerned with creating a working environment in which individual and team problems are anticipated, dealt with and resolved in a proactive and progressive manner. Many line managers get thrown in at the deep end of industrial relations where they have to deal with trade union representatives or staff associations. Good industrial relations are vital for organisations but if managers wait for problems to come to them, then they will not enjoy the benefits that a more proactive approach brings.

The achievement of good industrial relations will not necessarily make for good employee relations but the reverse is in fact true — good employee relations will in the main make for good industrial relations.

This chapter deals with one model that line managers can use in their pursuit of enhanced employee relations within their unit/section/department. Focusing on the values and behaviours described below should ensure that line managers have a very direct positive influence on employee relations in their part of the organisation.

Panel 12.1

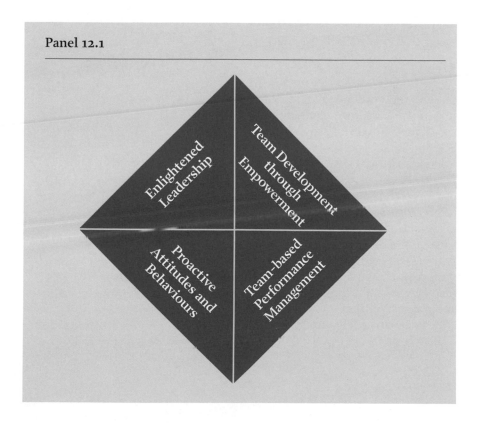

Enlightened Leadership

By enlightened leadership we mean incorporating some behaviours mentioned in the previous chapter, such as facilitative approaches within one's management style and inclusive visioning. Thus the enlightened leader takes an inclusive approach to developing a directional vision for the team. Utilising an inclusive approach to the development of vision gets the employees involved jointly with the manager in shaping the future of the work unit.

> Takes an inclusive approach to developing a directional vision for the team.

Enlightened leaders will also not just use the one management style for all individuals or teams. They will choose a style appropriate to organisational situations. In particular this appropriate style is related to the level of maturity or organisational experience that organisations/teams possess. Thus a line manager may take a strong interventionist approach with people who are new to the team's way of working but should stand back in a less interventionist style with those who are quite experienced in organisational processes.

Panel 12.2

Tips for Leadership Style

→ Be sure you do not have a 'one style fits all' approach

→ Base your style on the needs of the individual/team

→ Be directive when the need arises, likewise be facilitative in situations that allow for it

→ Discuss the appropriateness of your style with the team

→ Do not block others from being able to take on some of your leadership role.

Team Development through Empowerment

The behaviours that are pertinent to Team Development are:

→ Developing an attitude of letting go, as mentioned in the last chapter

→ Explaining to team members the nature of team development and working with them to identify further ways in which they can move forward as a team.

→ Allowing the team as much as possible to go about its own business for designing control elements into their work

→ Putting in place the enabling conditions for success - a critical activity required by managers

→ Reviewing with the team the work that they have done so that the team's own review skills are developed

It is worth noting that such development through empowerment may lead to some mistakes being made and it is important that individuals or teams are not punished if a mistake is made. Ensuring that this kind of punishment is not part of the culture will greatly aid the encouragement of calculated risk taking.

Team-based Performance Management

In a previous chapter, we discussed performance management with individual team members. We specifically highlighted the need for all managers to have a robust personal approach. They need to bring the same behaviours and skills to managing team performance.

Panel 12.3

Tips for Team-based Performance Management

→ Involve all team members in the process

→ Share with them all the information you have

→ Help them to articulate the context in terms of Strengths, Weaknesses, Opportunities and Threats facing the work of the team

→ Agree KRAs and challenging (but SMART) goals for the team

→ Determine who has responsibility (shared or personal) for each of the goals

→ Agree reporting and review mechanisms

→ Be prepared to celebrate successes throughout the year.

Proactive Attitudes and Behaviours

Very often line managers are accused of sitting back and waiting for things to happen but, in the cause of improved employee relations, we encourage as much proactivity as possible for managers on key issues of interest to employees. See Panel 12.4 for three areas of proactivity that really make a difference.

Panel 12.4

Three Areas for Proactive Behaviours

Team grievances	As we said in Chapter 6, a good line manager does not wait for grievances to develop. They are sufficiently proactive that they anticipate problems before they are spoken of by the team. This mode of thinking allows the line manager to tackle the grievance before it gets to a point of frustration for the individual and/or team.
Communications	A second example of proactive behaviour is in the area of communications where team members are often left in the dark for too long. A line manager behaving in a proactive mode attempts to ascertain as often as possible the information needs of the team. He or she promotes two-way communications by informing and involving the team to the maximum extent possible.
Team renewal	Proactive managers do not operate with a 'if it ain't broke don't fix it' mentality. They look at all dimensions of team effectiveness such as vision, values, goals, roles and processes to address areas which are dysfunctional and to identify improvements which can be made.

The above three examples of proactive attitudes and behaviour highlight the need for managers to focus on the team as a dynamic resource that needs to be cared for, maintained and developed.

This chapter was concerned with creating a positive employee relations climate. Much of the discussion centred on the manager taking a proactive approach, anticipating problems and planning for developments. In this way, a manager can move forward in a positive environment rather than having to operate in an institutionalised industrial relations context.

Summary of Chapter 12

→ Good industrial relations don't make good employee relations

→ Good employee relations in the main make for good industrial relations

→ Thus managers need to pursue with vigour good employee relations

→ The following model assists this process

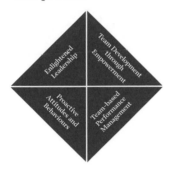

→ Enlightened leaders develop inclusive visioning and employ a range of leadership styles

→ Team development enhances team skills and builds good relationships

→ Team-based Performance Management clarifies expectations and develops relationships through regular feedback

→ Proactive positive approaches to employee concerns is noticed and helps deliver good Employee Relations.

13

Culture as an Aid to Organisational Strategy

Chapter outline

→ Culture: Building the Sort of Organisation You Want
→ Culture Explained
→ Building Blocks of Culture
→ Impact of Culture
→ Developing a Positive Culture
→ Time to Change Culture

Culture: Building the Sort of Organisation You Want

Over the years there have been hundreds of articles and books written about organisational culture. It is clearly an important phenomenon. It has been called the cement that holds an organisation together and is the most important source of competitive advantage that an organisation can achieve. It is sometimes referred to as the accumulated learning of an organisation about what it needs to do to survive and grow.

> Sociologists define culture as the values, beliefs and norms of behaviour of a group of people whether they are a nation, a tribe, a government department or a business organisation.

The central part of this chapter describes what a manager must do to develop a culture that will provide the basis for success in the future. It starts by defining culture and discussing the different types of culture. It looks at the impact of culture and how it can be a powerful force on which to build a successful organisation. The chapter concludes with actions a manager should take when the culture goes out of date and is no longer relevant to the needs of an organisation or its stakeholders.

Culture Explained

Sociologists define culture as the values, beliefs and norms of behaviour of a group of people whether they are a nation, a tribe, a government department or a business organisation. It is put more simply as 'the way we do things around here'. The culture of a business is set initially by the founders of a business who decide what business they are in and how they intend to succeed. Usually they define also how they will relate to the various stakeholders in the organisation such as their customers, their employees and the community they operate in. They decide on the service they will provide, how they will compete and the sort of behaviours they will reward.

As time passes, the organisation matures as it learns which behaviours are the ones that pay off for it. Values and beliefs develop which become generalised guidelines for shaping the ways in which the organisation operates. These are the building blocks of culture, as shown in Panel 13.1.

Panel 13.1

Building Blocks of Culture

Values: these are the most strongly held tenets that an organisation has about what is necessary for the organisation to succeed. Values are often defined in terms of Finance, Quality, Customer Service, People, Professionalism and Innovation.

Values are sometimes summed up in catch phrases such as 'The Customer is King", "Right First Time' and 'Employer of Choice'.

Beliefs: in cultural terms these operate best when they refer to key processes which an organisation believes are necessary to makes its values a reality.

Examples of beliefs include Six Sigma, Lean Manufacturing, No Quibble Guarantees and Employee Share Ownership.

Norms of behaviours: these are the visible manifestations of the values and beliefs and are sometimes referenced in comments about 'walking the talk'.

Behaviours are immediately apparent and can be seen in how people interact with their clients and customers, how they handle problems and how they relate to each other.

The interaction of the three building blocks referred to Panel 13.1 is key to the impact of culture on the success of an organisation.

Impact of Culture

All organisations have culture. However, culture does not have the same level of impact on their success or failure. Three factors determine the impact:

→ **Direction:** to what extent is the culture complementary to the strategy of the organisation and what it is trying to achieve? Some organisations have strongly held values and

beliefs that are not relevant to the success of an organisation. For example, an organisation may invest heavily in providing personal service when all their clients want is functional facilities. Likewise an organisation may provide terms and conditions of employment for its staff which do not relate to the service provided to its customers.

→ **Strength:** this dimension of culture relates to the extent to which an organisation is truly committed to a value. It is best seen in the extent to which it commits resources or makes sacrifices in relation to a value. No quibble money back guarantees could be costly but demonstrate an organisation's commitment to its customers. A good test of the strength of a culture occurs during difficult times when decisions are more challenging.

→ **Pervasiveness:** this dimension assesses the extent to which a culture extends the length and breadth of an organisation. There is no point in training front-line staff in delivering excellent customer service if other parts of the organisation, e.g. customer accounts, are failing to meet the same standards.

It is easy for organisations to draw up value statements which look good on the wall in the Reception Area but are not seen in the reality of day-to-day work. There is often a difference between espoused culture and the actual culture of the organisation. Panel 13.2 below shows a framework for linking values, beliefs and norms of behaviour. Different organisations have different ways of making the values a reality. The important point is to operate in a coherent, consistent manner that converts values into behaviours on the ground.

Panel 13.2

Values	Beliefs	Norms of behaviour
Innovation	Research	% of revenues devoted to research No. of PhDs hired
Low cost	Lean manufacturing Management accounting	Continuous improvement programmes Outsourcing of non-core activities
Employer of choice	Employee involvement Staff development	Monthly meetings with all staff Percentage of payroll devoted to training each year
Execution	Performance Planning and Review Incentives	Goal-setting Regular feedback on performance Rewards linked to performance

Unless an organisation can demonstrate the linkage between these elements, it is likely to miss out on 'walking the talk'. Managers who want to develop a culture which supports their goals need to align the various values, beliefs and norms of behaviour so that they deliver concrete results. This approach works best when standards of performance are set for the norms of behaviour.

Developing a Positive Culture

Fundamentally it is the manager's responsibility to develop an appropriate culture for his or her workgroup. Managers who want a culture that positively reinforces the work that they are trying to deliver, must be passionate about the values and beliefs. They need to be clear about the sort of organisation they want, be able to articulate it and then use every opportunity to reinforce the values, beliefs and behaviours that will deliver the required culture. People need to see the sacrifices their managers are prepared to make if they are to believe in the values as real and enduring for their organisation.

Managers who wish to pursue culture should become acutely aware of the power of the behaviours and artifacts outlined below:

→ **Leadership:** Managers should show their personal commitment to the values by everything they say and do.

They need to be exemplars of the values by leading from the front and being prepared to sacrifice short-term goals in order to benefit from the long term benefits which the values will bring. The most obvious sign of commitment by managers is seen in the time they personally commit e.g. by attending the launch of a new programme by participating in the delivery of training programmes and by providing all of the enabling conditions that will support those values.

→ **Communications:** Managers who want to develop a good culture, talk constantly about the values and behaviours that they expect from themselves and their team. They use a plethora of events to reinforce the values such as at induction programmes, team meetings and company social activities.

→ **Symbols** and symbolic behaviour are important mechanisms for demonstrating values. Turning their office into a meeting room is one way in which a manager can demonstrate that he or she values team-working over their own personal status.

→ **Selecting and promoting people** who share the values is essential in order to build the culture of an organisation.

→ **Training and development** processes are vital in helping people to understand the rationale and reality behind

105

values, to learn the language of the culture e.g. the true meaning of teamwork, and to develop the know-how and skills associated with translating the culture into their everyday work.

→ **Reward systems** should look not only at performance but also at the work behaviours of team members. They send a strong message to team members if, for example, a successful sales person finds that rewards are limited if his or her behaviours do not support a team ethos or where the performance is at the expense of customer service.

→ **Corrective action** may be necessary where a team member consistently demonstrates behaviours at variance with the culture of the organisation.

Time to Change Culture

One of the problems with strong cultures is that sometimes they look backwards rather than forwards. A changed marketplace may require different solutions to those that worked well in the past. In recent years, the airline industry found that customers value cost efficiency more than they do personal services.

It is important that managers provide the lead in identifying changes in the operating environment as early as possible so as to provide time for the culture to change. It is important not to throw the baby out with the bath water. Sometimes it is not necessary to change the value but simply to change the belief systems related to the organisational values. Take for example two organisations which had values around excellence in design. Nokia became a world leader in mobile phones by recognising that aesthetics were as important to customers as functionality. Motorola lost its lead in the marketplace by continuing to focus on the technology behind the design.

Summary of Chapter 13

→ Culture plays a vital part in the success of organisations

→ Value systems and beliefs are at the heart of organisational cultures

→ Managers are responsible for the development of an appropriate culture

→ They have a variety of tools at their disposal to develop and reinforce the appropriate culture

→ Sometimes a culture goes out of date and managers need to take appropriate action to change the culture

→ Translating values and beliefs into coherent behaviours is critical to culture development.

Notes

Notes

Notes

Notes

Notes

Notes

Further publications in 2011 and 2012

- → Managing Reward
- → Handling Discipline - *Best Practice*
- → Managing Diversity
- → Negotiating Skills
- → Burnout
- → Coaching Skills
- → Life Balance
- → Conflict Resolution
- → Influencing Skills
- → Mediation Skills
- → Assertiveness and Self-Esteem
- → Strategic Issue Communications
- → Personal Development
- → Innovation
- → Compliance
- → Strategy Development and Implementation
- → Leadership and Strategic Change
- → Managing with Impact - *Focusing on Performance through People*
- → Strategic Marketing
- → Entrepreneurial Skills
- → Managing Attendance at Work
- → Employee Relations
- → Improving your Writing Skills
- → Organisation Development/ Training
- → Change Management
- → Organisation Design
- → Energy Management
- → International Marketing
- → Governance in Today's Corporate World
- → Customer Relationship Management
- → Building Commitment to Quality
- → Understanding Finance
- → PR Skills for Managers
- → Logistics and Supply Chain
- → Dealing with Difficult People
- → Effective Meetings
- → Communication Skills
- → Facilitation Skills
- → Managing Upwards
- → Giving and Receiving Feedback
- → Consumer Behaviour
- → Delegation and Empowerment
- → Basic Economics for Managers
- → Finance for non Financial Executives
- → Business Forecasting
- → The Marketing of Services

ManagementBriefs.com
Essential Insights for Busy Managers

Our list of books already published includes:

→ Be Interview-Wise: *How to Prepare for and Manage Your Interviews*
Brian McIvor

→ HR for Line Managers: *Best Practice*
Frank Scott-Lennon & Conor Hannaway

→ Bullying & Harassment: *Values and Best Practice Responses*
Frank Scott-Lennon & Margaret Considine

→ Career Detection: *Finding and Managing Your Career*
Brian McIvor

→ Impactful Presentations: *Best Practice Skills*
Yvonne Farrell

→ Managing Projects: *A Practical Guide*
Dermot Duff & John Quilliam

→ Marketing Skills: *A Practical Guide*
Garry Hynes & Ronan Morris

→ Performance Management: *Developing People and Performance*
Frank Scott-Lennon & Fergus Barry

→ Proven Selling Skills: *For Winners*
Ronan McNamara

→ Redundancy: *A Development Opportunity for You!*
Frank Scott-Lennon, Fergus Barry & Brian McIvor

→ Safety Matters!: *A Guide to Health and Safety at Work*
Adrian Flynn & John Shaw of Phoenix Safety

→ Time Matters: *Making the Most of Your Day*
Julia Rowan

→ Emotional Intelligence (EQ): *A Leadership Imperative!*
Daire Coffey & Deirdre Murray